Support for

"I don't remember how I discovered Adam Beck's book *Maximize Your Child's Bilingual Ability*. What I vividly remember, though, a few pages into the book, is the feeling that I was holding a gold nugget. It was the book I had been searching for for a long time. Previous books or information on raising bilingual children that I had found were too academic to be truly helpful on a day-to-day basis. My oldest child was 5 and I was really struggling with our bilingual journey. I needed real-life advice, not a lecture on the latest discoveries on brain development (fascinating, but it had led me nowhere). Alongside great tips to apply every day, the book is a source of enthusiasm and perseverance, which in my opinion is the reason why Adam's work differentiates itself from the rest of the literature on the topic. I recommend it to anyone who wants to raise their child bilingual. Half of the work in raising bilingual children is to keep going no matter what. On days where the motivation or energy dwindles, I open the book and recharge. The best way I could describe it is a down-to-earth, fun, invigorating guide full of optimism that will leave you feeling like you can move mountains."

—*Elise in the U.S., originally from France*

"Adam's book *Maximize Your Child's Bilingual Ability* is the best thing I've ever read about bilingualism. I love how practical it is, not just focusing on the different studies and data on the subject, but giving the reader a lot of practical ideas on what to do and how. It's so thorough, I've read it more than once. I can't recommend it enough. His forum, The Bilingual Zoo, has allowed me to get in touch with other families in similar situations as my own. This helps immensely, not just because we can share what works for us and the different resources we use, but because it allows us to feel like we aren't alone on this journey. This forum is my go-to online place whenever I have any free time. His blog, Bilingual Monkeys, has also helped our family with different ideas and resources. I've checked it many times for inspiration or resources."

—*Raquel in Spain*

"I've read a number of blogs about raising bilingual kids and Bilingual Monkeys is the best! As I'm a thorough person, I read every single post, from the very beginning, and I felt as if you were speaking directly to me. So I've followed the progress of your kids and your parenting and it's been eye-opening and inspiring. Taking your blog as a whole, I'm struck by your reverence for life itself, your carpe diem attitude, and your exuberance, joy, and creativity. I like your sense of humor and how your blog posts are interspersed with light comic relief, while also getting across the serious messages and research that you've done. In terms of the impact, well, it has been life-changing for me as you've encouraged me firstly to not give up hope, then to persevere."

—*Vaishali in the UK*

"The Bilingual Monkeys website is such a wonderful resource and I'm grateful I found it at the beginning of our bilingual journey. Your book, especially, gave me a path to follow and motivation that it can really work. I also feel like I have tools to use when our minority language needs a boost. There have been so many times that I have gone to the forum to look up certain issues or checked the website for specific articles. I pass on the link to both the website and book to anyone who will take it! Thank you, Adam, for being such a practical and positive leader in the bilingual community!"

—*Heidi in Germany, originally from the U.S.*

"I read Adam's book and also communicated with him personally about my concerns involving speech delay in my bilingual son Jack (3.5 years old, Russian and English). Adam's knowledge and dedication to the subject was very impressive, and proved to be very helpful for me. I followed his advice, and now our son is fluent in both languages. I think Adam's work is extremely important, and I will support him in whatever he does, since I believe that without language you cannot access the treasure of cultural traditions."

—*Elaine in the U.S., originally from Russia*

"I have two fully bilingual children (German/English, 5 and 3) and besides my own efforts as a parent, I owe that exclusively to you. Honestly, if I hadn't stumbled across your work, I wouldn't have started raising them that way. I'm not a native speaker of English, so I always thought it would be 'impossible,' yes, 'inappropriate' for me to even attempt raising bilingual children. I read a few books and articles on the topic of child bilingualism, but it was reading your book, specifically, that gave me lots and lots of practical ideas when I didn't even know where to begin. It gave me perspective. It encouraged me. And it was reading stories of other parents in similar circumstances at The Bilingual Zoo forum that made me understand that my own language skills don't have to be a deal breaker. Your book *Maximize Your Child's Bilingual Ability*, the forum, and your blog, taken together, give me a sense of community, a feeling of being understood and not alone. And while I'm still very aware of my own limitations, I walk this journey together with many others and my children's language skills continue to thrive. So thank you for being out there and for doing what you're doing!"

—*Angelika in Austria*

"I came across your book when I was pregnant with my daughter. I used your book for a post graduate project on bilingualism, for my personal life, and for my work supporting bilingual families, children in schools, and teachers. I have recommended your book, blog, YouTube channel, and other resources to everyone I have encountered on this path. Thanks so much for your hard work in this quest. Infinitely grateful, amigo!"

—*Silvia in Scotland, originally from Spain*

"Adam's books and advice have made an amazing impact on our entire family. I started reading his work before I gave birth to my daughter almost five years ago, and have been following him ever since. My daughter is now trilingual (Italian, English, Spanish) like her mom, and is now learning to read in all three languages as well. With the guidance of Adam's wisdom, my husband, who studied Spanish in school but never became fluent, now speaks Italian at an intermediate level and is also working daily on his Spanish. We will continue to implement Adam's advice with our son, who will turn 1 in a couple of weeks. Thank you, Adam, for all that you do; you are a gift to the world!"

—*Bruna in the U.S., originally from Italy*

BILINGUAL SUCCESS STORIES
Around the World

Parents Raising Multilingual Kids Share
Their Experiences and Encouragement

ADAM BECK

Author of *Maximize Your Child's Bilingual Ability*

Bilingual Adventures
Hiroshima, Japan

For my parents,
and parents everywhere

Contents

Contact Information

Many of the parents featured in this book have provided contact information so that readers may reach out to them directly. When it's available, this information—which was current at the time this book was published—appears at the end of each family's story.

Also, please feel free to contact me personally if I can be of further support beyond my books, my blog, my forum, and my social media pages. I'm always happy to hear from parents and I'd be glad to cheer on your family, too, toward even greater success and joy.

✉ adam@bilingualmonkeys.com

🌐 bilingualmonkeys.com (blog)

🌐 bilingualzoo.com (forum)

▶ youtube.com/bilingualmonkeys

f facebook.com/bilingualmonkeys

⊙ @bilingualadventures

🐦 @bilingualmonkey

Key Terms

As used in this book, the "majority language" is the main language of a particular country or community; the "minority language" is the language that is not used as widely within that country or community. While "minority language" will generally be used in the singular in this book, please consider it shorthand for any number of minority languages within a family. In the same way, "bilingual" will often refer more broadly to multiple languages, whether two, three, or more, thus also embracing the terms "trilingual" and "multilingual" under the "bilingual" banner.

Foreword:
Kudos to the bilingual
family story collector!

by Annick De Houwer, PhD
Director, the Harmonious Bilingualism Network
(habilnet.org)

With few exceptions, children everywhere learn the language that is used at their preschool and school. Things are different for any other language children may hear at home. Regardless of how important that language is in the world at large, it is at a disadvantage. Compared to the language used in school and public life (the local "majority" language), children may have trouble developing any other language they hear at home. Locally, that language is a "minority" language.

You won't get far with English, the world's global language, in the French-speaking Walloon region of Belgium—few people will understand you, and you can't apply for any social benefits or pay your taxes in English. In Wallonia, English is a minority language. Children who hear English at home in Wallonia may not learn to speak it and may only speak French, the majority language. While their English-speaking parents may understand French, their English-speaking grandparents and other relatives often do not. This is often heartbreaking for all involved. The English-speaking parents may feel ashamed towards their own parents in Britain for not managing to raise children who can speak with their grandparents. Parents may also feel resentful towards their children for not speaking their language, and when the children grow up they may in turn blame their parents for not making sure that they learned to speak (and read and write) English. These families are not experiencing harmonious bilingualism.

Fortunately, harmonious bilingualism, where family members are all happy with how things are working out with regard to language, is quite attainable. We know from research that many parents who speak a minority language at home with their children can and do raise bilingual children who are able to understand and speak both a minority and a majority language. The engaging book you're about to read focuses on parents who are successfully raising children who are fluent in a minority language spoken at home.

The book tells the stories of 26 families from across the globe, from China through Poland to California, representing scores of minority languages, from Mongolian in Denmark to Hindi in the United States. The stories tell of dedication, effort, perseverance, and love—love for minority languages, and, above all, for the children who speak them.

Of course, the stories in this book did not magically appear out of nowhere—they were collected by Adam Beck, himself a parent in a bilingual family in Japan. For many years, Adam has been working with and for bilingual families everywhere, through his website, forum, books and more. He managed to gain the trust of countless bilingual families worldwide. It is much to his credit that so many families allowed him intimate access to their bilingual family life.

Not only did Adam manage to collect many in-depth bilingual family stories. He weaves those stories together into one big story showing how, thanks to a lot of loving work from parents, children can grow into confident and happy users of several languages. Kudos to the bilingual family story collector!

Rixensart, April 2021

Introduction

I f you're reading this book, chances are you have a deeply felt desire to experience as much success as possible on your bilingual journey with your children. The success stories in these pages, shared by a wide range of families in many parts of the world, reveal the kinds of attitudes and actions that can help empower your family to enjoy the same sort of rewarding success. In other words, the focus of this book is on the *actual practice* of raising children to acquire active ability in more than one language, conveyed through the lived experiences of parents who are now succeeding admirably at their bilingual aim.

While every family is, of course, very different, the fact remains that the fundamental challenge of raising bilingual children is largely the same, no matter the location or languages or lifestyle. In a nutshell, it involves providing effective support for the family's minority language throughout the years of childhood.

Effective support for the minority language means that the child receives ample exposure to this target language, whether from parents or other sources of input, and feels an organic need to use that language actively.

The more language exposure the child receives, in interactive and engaging ways, and the more need the child feels to use that language actively, the more success can be experienced as the bilingual journey proceeds.

(This may not always be an overt need, however. Some parents with obvious proficiency in the majority language are still able to "condition" their children to use the minority language by nurturing a feeling of need through the emotional bond that they establish in this language, as certain stories in this book demonstrate.)

Therefore, the two "core conditions" for raising a bilingual child with active ability in the minority language are *exposure* and *need*, for without effectively satisfying these conditions, the child will likely not receive enough exposure, or feel enough need, to develop capable and confident ability in this language.

Exposure and need, then, form the deepest thread that stretches throughout this book, tying together the varied lives of these bilingual and multilingual families. None of the families in this book are "perfect" when it comes to the two "core conditions," but they have each satisfied these conditions to a sufficient degree so that the children have been able to develop active ability in the minority language. Being "perfect" in our efforts is not only impossible, it's unnecessary for experiencing significant success.

The joy of success

While this book emphasizes the general idea of success as enabling the child to grow toward using the minority language actively and freely, to me, a successful outcome alone is not enough for a bilingual journey to truly be called a "success story." As I've stressed in my writing over the years, the process itself should also feel as joyful as possible for both parent and child. In other words, our larger goal is not only success at language acquisition, but language acquisition through joyful experiences. Again, there is no perfection when it comes to success or joy; our aim should simply be to maximize both to the extent we realistically can.

Thus, the success stories in this book not only point toward how families can experience success in their goal of bilingual development, they also highlight the idea of making the daily process itself as joyful as we can manage. Ultimately, it is this joy—and the general well-being within the family it brings—that makes the longer journey not only more pleasurable but also more productive when it comes to nurturing language acquisition.

My own story

My own story as a parent of bilingual children has been blessed by the sort of success and joy being realized by the families in this book. I share that story, as well as my experiences as a longtime teacher of bilingual children, in my book *Maximize Your Child's Bilingual Ability*. When I wrote that book, my children were 11 and 8; today they are 17 and 14. For me and my family, the bilingual journey is now largely over, and my main goal has been accomplished. This doesn't mean that I'm lounging in my hammock just yet; I continue to pursue the efforts I can to advance their bilingual ability. But it's also true that, as children grow older and become more independent, our time with them, and our influence on their lives, shrinks sharply. Looking back, I'm grateful that I was able to make the most of their younger days when this time and influence were most abundant.

Over the years I've been privileged to cross paths with many families out in the world who hold a bilingual or multilingual aim, intersections that have come mainly through virtual interactions at my blog, Bilingual Monkeys; my forum, The Bilingual Zoo; social media; email; and video chats. And though, in most cases, I haven't had the opportunity to meet the parents and their children in person, the truth is, I've gotten closer to many of these people than I have to the people around me in "real life." The distinction, I think, is the fact that, even though these friends out in the world and I lead very different lives, our bilingual goal for our children is such a central and meaningful part of our being that we feel a direct kinship on this deeper level. At the same time, the kinds of daily challenges that this goal brings, and the emotional ups and downs that are part and parcel of the process, enable us to connect in ways that often feel far more significant than our interactions with others in our more immediate surroundings.

It was through these friendships, and through the experiences that parents have shared with me, that I became fascinated by the story of each family I encountered, how each family is so uniquely different and yet the elements for success and joy at this aim are so profoundly similar. Eventually, then, I became determined to capture at least some of these appealing stories in a book that could offer encouraging examples for other families undertaking the same fulfilling mission.

Developing this book

In all, I was able to interview over 40 parents, most individually but some as couples. About half of these in-depth interviews took place in person and about half were conducted virtually. During the fall of 2019 I traveled through Europe and enjoyed short homestays with a number of bilingual and multilingual families. It was a marvelous opportunity to spend time with the parents and children in their homes, meetings that not only provided a wealth of material for this book, they left me with glowing memories.

In fact, after that trip, I had hoped to take further trips out into the world, to meet as many families in person as I realistically could... but the coronavirus pandemic which erupted just months later made this impossible. And so, like the rest of the world, I turned to online avenues, like Skype and Zoom, to continue conducting interviews. (Since most of the interviews were done pre-pandemic, the content of the book doesn't generally reflect the pandemic conditions that have affected these families in various ways. Language exposure out in the community, and from travel, has obviously been curtailed, but many parents have mentioned a bright silver lining in the fact that they have been able to spend more quality time with their kids, and put more emphasis on the minority language, while at home amid this time of restrictions.)

I very much regret not being able to include the full story of every family I spoke with, but, of course, the needs of the book itself had to be taken into account, including the need to keep the book to a reasonable length. I remain deeply grateful to all these families, however, whether or not their story appears in the final version. All of them have experienced much success and joy in their journeys and it was an honor, truly, to speak with them so personally about their lives.

The stories that make up this book were selected based on a range of factors that include:

- the family's location

- where the parents are from originally

- the family's languages

- the ages of the children (in the book, children's ages are noted in years and months at the time the interview took place, such as "3.9" or "11.5")

- the family's particular circumstances

- aspects of their experience that highlight important principles

Of course, a book like this is unable to represent every country or language or situation, but I have sought to offer as wide a range of families as I realistically could, given the natural constraints of this task. Along with families that might be considered more "traditional" when thinking of bilingual families—such as an international couple with two different native languages—there are also the stories of families in which the parent or parents are non-native speakers of the minority language, a single parent raising a multilingual child, a bilingual child with special needs, and more. I realize that readers may wish that I had included other scenarios as well, but I ask for your understanding with regard to this daunting challenge of being as "inclusive" as possible in a book about families across the world. Perhaps a second book along these lines can continue to expand our perspective of the world's bilingual and multilingual families.

Writing this book

The 26 stories in this book have been arranged in a roughly chronological fashion, from families with younger children to families with older children (who may also have younger children). The intent behind this structure is to convey the broad sweep of bilingualism, from birth to the older teenage years—and even, finally, into multiple generations—so that readers not only gain insight into the ongoing efforts and progress within the day-to-day lives of bilingual families, they also glimpse the greater arc of the bilingual journey itself, in its entirety, and how success and joy can serve as the through line of this years-long experience.

These stories are necessarily "snapshots in time" of the particular moment when I interviewed the parents about their experience. Since the day these interviews were conducted, the children and their language ability have naturally continued to grow and new challenges have arisen. For the most part, though, I have consciously avoided revising these "snapshots" with updates from months later because, of course, since the lives of these families are constantly evolving, such revisions could carry on without end. In some cases, though, I do include brief follow-up comments in my afterword that concludes each account.

In writing these stories, I drew on the transcripts of the recorded interviews, sometimes seeking further information in subsequent exchanges. The quoted portions have been taken directly from these transcripts, with light editing as needed, and the final version of the text for each family's story was approved by the parents. (In some cases, parents asked that I use pseudonyms for the names of family members, to help protect their privacy, but the stories themselves are frank and factual accounts.)

As the writer, my intention was to strike an effective balance between allowing the story to "tell itself," for readers to draw their own conclusions, while also emphasizing and expanding on certain points that I believe are particularly important to highlight, including in my short afterword. At the same time, I tried to make each story concise and engaging so that busy parents will find the text accessible and enjoyable to read while benefiting from the wealth of relevant, real-world information that the book contains.

In short, I have done my best to create the most practical, empowering book of "success stories" I could for parents with a bilingual or multilingual aim. From my experience with *Maximize Your Child's Bilingual Ability*, however, I recognize that no book can be all things to all people, particularly when it comes to such a broad subject like raising bilingual children. Still, I hope this book will resonate with you and leave you with lingering value that can make a difference in your own journey with your family. If the stories that follow can enhance the success and joy that you experience with your children, to even a modest degree, it will have served its purpose and I, along with the families that have generously shared their experiences with us, will be very pleased.

With my best bilingual wishes,

Adam Beck
Hiroshima, Japan

The Early Childhood Years

The first stage of the journey involves providing as much exposure to the minority language as possible, from as early as possible, with the main aim of "conditioning" the child to communicate in that language once he or she begins to speak. While a child can develop proficiency in an additional language at any age—languages can be acquired consecutively rather than simultaneously—when parents are able to make the most of the first few formative years, these proactive efforts can establish a firm and active foundation in the target language which may then be more smoothly sustained through the subsequent years of childhood.

1

Single Parent Nurtures Early Multilingual Success

- ▶ Marisa is originally from Spain and now lives in the U.S.
- ▶ She is a professor of Spanish at a university in the state of Virginia.
- ▶ A single mother, she has a daughter, Laura, who is 3.2 years old.
- ▶ Their majority language is English and their minority languages are Spanish, German, and French.

This book begins with the story of a single parent nurturing four languages with a 3-year-old child. The success that Marisa is experiencing with Laura is an encouraging example for all parents, no matter the make-up of the family, because the overarching truth is that *any* family can experience a great deal of success at a bilingual or multilingual aim over the years of childhood as long as there is sufficient persistence.

In fact, this is the basic "secret" to success that underpins the whole experience: persistence from day to day, and perseverance over the years. There may be vast differences among the families in this book, and out in the world, but what unites us in our aim is the determination to keep going, to keep trying, to persevere for the payoff.

And remember, there is *always* a payoff to perseverance.

Dreaming of a bilingual child

Marisa first dreamed of being a mother, and raising a bilingual child, when she was just 12.

She had begun learning English not long before, and liked the language, but she was growing up in Spain and assumed she would live there in the future, too. "I thought Spanish would be the majority language and English the minority language," she recalled.

Marisa is from a family of teachers who are monolingual in Spanish, and Marisa herself was monolingual until the day she began studying English at the age of 11. She quickly took an interest in the language and made strong progress through middle school and high school.

She then majored in English in college and imagined that she would eventually become a teacher at a university in Spain. "I didn't want to be a high school teacher because those kids would have killed me!" she explained with a laugh, among the many trills of laughter that grace her fluent English.

However, in her last year of college, one of her professors suggested that she teach Spanish in the U.S. for a year to further strengthen her English ability and make her more marketable after returning to Spain.

So Marisa went to the U.S. in 1996.

And still lives there today.

Pursuing a new career path

While Marisa enjoyed her first teaching assignment, at a small college in Illinois, she realized that she needed more formal training in teaching Spanish if she wanted to continue in this field. "I had studied to be an English teacher," she said. "I had never taught my native language. My students would ask about things and I was like, I have no idea how to explain that!" So she went on to enroll at a large university in Illinois, where she earned her MA and PhD in Hispanic Linguistics with a certification in Second Language Acquisition and Teacher Education.

In 2005, Marisa then moved to Virginia to become a professor of Spanish at a university there.

And in 2016, Laura was born.

Giving her daughter a multilingual gift

Because her parents don't speak English, Marisa was determined to foster her daughter's Spanish side. "She had to bond with my mom," she said, the resolve evident in her voice. "And she could only do that in Spanish."

Spanish, then, is the main minority language, and her highest priority: the aim is "native level" ability in this language. At the same time, Marisa has been eager to give Laura an early start in other languages, too. The initial impulse for this, though, differs from the deeply felt desire she holds to hand down Spanish as a heritage language.

"German and French began from a more practical perspective," she explained. "Because I'm a single mother, I was thinking, 'Oh my god, oh my god, how am I going to save money for her college education?' Then somebody told me, 'Did you know that college in Germany is free?' And I said, 'Free? You just got me at free!'"

Marisa, in fact, studied German when she was younger, though she hadn't used this language in some time. German thus became the second minority language. And French, though she speaks little of this language herself, became the third as she hopes to send Laura to a school, from kindergarten, which includes both Spanish and French as part of its curriculum.

While some people express surprise that a 3-year-old is actively acquiring four languages, wondering if this is too many, Marisa maintains a healthy perspective on their multilingual journey. She stressed that English and Spanish are their main two languages and need the strongest proficiency. At the same time, as long as Laura continues to enjoy her experience of German and French, Marisa will nurture her progress in these languages as well, to whatever level can be achieved. "The more proficiency she can get in these languages, too, the better for her," she said.

Though introducing German and French may have been prompted by more practical concerns, Marisa has come to view the value of her daughter's emerging multilingual ability in a broader light. "Foreign languages have opened a lot of doors for me and I want to give my daughter that same gift. And the best time to begin learning them is when she's little."

Emphasizing their minority languages

Ever since this journey began, Marisa has been very consistent about speaking to Laura in Spanish and (sometimes) German. She has also actively supplemented the language exposure from her own speech with input from other speakers of Spanish, German, and French. Along with input from her family in Spain—at a distance and in person during return visits—she has arranged for students from her university to interact with her daughter in these languages.

At the same time, Marisa has proactively sought to emphasize books, music, videos, and other resources in these minority languages while mindfully limiting the influence of English inside the house.

"The only English she hears at home comes from the alarm system, twice a day, when we turn it on and off. I even wanted to change this to Spanish, but it didn't have that option!"

In addition to the daily efforts she makes to nurture her daughter's development in Spanish, German, and French, Marisa also takes full advantage of her long vacations as a university teacher and returns to Spain twice a year—for about two months in the summer and one month in the winter—so Laura can spend time with family members and benefit from the immersion of these visits.

Trusting her acquisition of English, too

Meanwhile, Laura attends daycare from 8:30 to 3:30, so is also immersed in English for many hours each day. The teachers have told Marisa that, initially, her daughter tried to communicate in Spanish but has since come to use English. Marisa, though, is still unsure how well Laura speaks this language because she will rarely use it in her presence.

"I'm her Kryptonite," Marisa laughed. "The moment I'm around, English is gone. She doesn't speak it, even when everybody else is speaking it. Oh, every now and then she'll say a word in English when I'm there, but it's very limited. And when she says a word in English, she's then nice enough to give me the Spanish translation in case I didn't understand!"

While Laura is surely becoming more conscious of the fact that her mother is proficient in English, too, Marisa hasn't yet experienced any difficulty in maintaining their communication in Spanish.

She attributes this to the emotional bond that she has established with her daughter in their minority languages, especially in Spanish.

At this point, too, she isn't concerned about Laura's English side because she trusts that the ongoing exposure she's receiving in this language at daycare, and at school in the future, will fuel satisfactory development.

Overcoming moments of doubt

Marisa admits, though, to having had moments of doubt when it comes to the minority languages.

"The difficult part of this is that there's no immediate feedback," she said, pointing out how the first couple of years, before the child starts to speak, can be a psychological test for first-time parents. "We've become used to wanting immediate results, but language acquisition isn't like that."

She mentioned a friend who she felt gave up on his bilingual aim too soon because this friend didn't think his efforts were paying off.

Her understanding of language development, though, hasn't shielded her from experiencing similar feelings. "I'm a linguist and I know how this works, but I'm also a mom and so at some point the mom brain takes over the linguist brain and I get worried about things that I know I shouldn't be worried about."

At one point, Marisa herself nearly gave up on the idea of nurturing German and French. A student had come to her office to read German books to Laura, but the little girl was running about and making a mess instead. "I thought, 'What the hell am I doing? She's not even paying attention.'"

But Marisa understood the value of this early language exposure, and trusted that these efforts would indeed eventually pay off. "My linguist brain won out over my frustrated mom brain," she said. "And now, now is when I'm starting to see the results."

Marisa reports that Laura's ability in Spanish is quite good for her young age, and she also has growing ability in both German and French. In fact, this multilingual journey with her daughter is also enabling Marisa to improve her own German and French at the same time.

Experiencing the journey as a single parent

Asked about her experience pursuing a multilingual aim as a single parent, Marisa said that it might have been a "different scenario" if a partner had been present and speaking English every day, which could have diluted Laura's exposure to Spanish and the other languages and potentially undercut her need to actively use them.

"Spanish is definitely her strongest language. When she wakes up in the middle of the night, it's all Spanish. It comes naturally to her at this point. I haven't had any issues with her not speaking the minority language." She added with a laugh, "But I don't know if I should tell people, 'If you want to raise a bilingual child, don't get married! Stay single!'"

As for the downsides of her experience, Marisa mentioned the challenges of being a single parent, in general, but said that this hasn't really presented any particular difficulties when it comes to Laura's language development. On the contrary, as she noted, it seems she has been able to emphasize the minority languages very effectively during these early formative years of her daughter's life.

Making the process engaging and enjoyable

Sharing some advice for other parents with a bilingual or multilingual aim, Marisa said, "Be very, very persistent. It's like learning to play an instrument. You have to keep going to see the results."

She acknowledged, though, that, as parents, we sometimes have a hard time judging how persistent we should be, and particularly if the child is showing some resistance to our efforts. This is why, she went on, the child's experience of the learning process must also be engaging and enjoyable. Without enough engagement, enough enjoyment, persistence becomes too pushy.

While Marisa is deeply pleased with her daughter's multilingual progress to date, she also recognizes that there will likely be challenges ahead as English grows more dominant in Laura's life. Still, she pledged to do her best to advance their minority languages, adding with a laugh, "I'm happy to continue being the English Kryptonite!"

AFTERWORD: I spoke with Marisa again during the pandemic and she told me that because Laura had not been attending school—and, consequently, had not been receiving that daily exposure to English—she decided to permit a bit more English at home. Marisa's action in this way is a good example of how parents must remain flexible and evolve in their efforts as their circumstances evolve...and this has been true of so many parents, worldwide, since the outbreak of the coronavirus in early 2020. At the same time, Marisa's decision is also a good example of how such choices should be carried out in thoughtful and strategic ways. In her words: "I only speak English when I'm wearing my baseball cap. And she's pretty good with that. If she feels like speaking a little English, she asks me to put it on. She never starts speaking in English on her own. In fact, if I happen to say an English word without the cap, she says to me in Spanish, 'Mom, you need the cap! You're speaking in English!'"

CONTACT & RESOURCES FOR MARISA

✉ mariaisabel.martinezmira@gmail.com

📖 *En tu Medio: Intermediate Spanish* (co-author of this Spanish textbook published by Wiley and Sons)

2

Music Inspires Joyful Engagement and Progress

- ▶ Richard is originally from the Czech Republic and his native language is Czech. He is a professional pianist and piano teacher at a university in China.

- ▶ His wife, Xingxing, is Chinese and grew up speaking both Mandarin and a local Chinese dialect. She is a professional singer of opera and other genres of music as well as a music teacher at the same university.

- ▶ Their daughter, Lada, is about to turn 3.

- ▶ Richard speaks Czech, their minority language, to Lada; Xingxing uses Mandarin, their majority language. The couple communicates with one another mainly in English.

Music is an important part of the success story of every family in this book, with music in the target language used both actively, through singing songs together, and passively, through playing music in the home and in the car.

For Richard and Xingxing, though, music serves as the main engine for their multilingual lifestyle and their multilingual aim for their daughter Lada, who is nearly 3. Music is not only a powerful source of exposure to their multiple languages, and has played a pivotal role in the strong start to their journey together, it is also a means of cultivating Lada's interest and joy in these languages.

Richard in the Czech Republic

As a boy in the Czech Republic, Richard attended a school with an emphasis on the arts and music. His love for music grew out of this early exposure at school along with the influence he experienced at home. "It was a pretty big house," Richard said, explaining that it was divided into three units for different generations of the family. "And in my grandmother's apartment, there was a piano so I also played piano there."

His grandmother not only set a musical example, she was a multilingual speaker herself. "She knew five languages, but she didn't know English," Richard said. "Nowadays I think it would be hard to find anyone who speaks five languages but can't speak English!" As a child, his grandmother was trilingual in Czech, Slovak, and Hungarian, then also learned German and French.

Richard admits that he didn't take after his grandmother when it came to language learning, at least early on. "I first started to learn German when I was 11, but I didn't enjoy it so I didn't learn anything. When I was 14, I started to learn English. My English probably got to an advanced level when I was 23 or 24. I was living with people from other countries at my university and I was often with them."

He continued, "I also learned some Spanish because I had a roommate from Mexico. I got really interested in Mexico and we traveled there to do a music project together."

He then turned to his wife and smiled. "I never thought of learning Chinese until I met Xingxing," he said, noting that he has reached an "upper-intermediate level" and uses Chinese on a daily basis when at work and out in the community.

Xingxing in China, New Zealand, and Germany

Half a world away, as Richard sat playing his grandmother's piano, Xingxing was playing the piano, too, in a large city in southwestern China. "In that area we spoke a dialect," she said. "It's actually close to Mandarin, but it has different tones. At school, we had to speak Mandarin so, basically, I grew up with two languages."

"So I started my piano lessons when I was 10," she said, "and my lessons were progressing really well." As she grew, however, her hands remained small and so her piano teacher recommended that she begin singing lessons instead.

Xingxing started learning English in school at the age of 13. At 17, she took part in an exchange program that brought her to New Zealand to complete her last year of high school. After graduating from high school, she continued her education in New Zealand at a music school then began singing and training at an opera house there. Eventually, she earned a scholarship that enabled her to study overseas and because she had developed a passion for German art songs—even winning a singing competition in this genre—she decided to go to Germany.

Xingxing spent nearly four years in Germany studying music and becoming proficient in German during this time. "I was almost finished with my studies," she said, "and I was taking advantage of all the possible opportunities to sing, going to singing competitions and auditions. I saw the poster for an international singing competition in the Czech Republic and I signed up. Then I just hopped on a train and went there."

"That's how we met," Richard said, explaining that, because Xingxing was one of the winners of the competition, she was then invited on a tour of 12 concerts, with Richard serving as an accompanist for the performers. "We were together for over a week of concerts, so that's how it started. If she hadn't gotten that award, we wouldn't have gotten together."

He added with a grin, "So like I always say, she actually won *me* in that competition."

While the couple hadn't initially planned on making a new life together in China, during a visit to Xingxing's family four years ago, they received some job offers and decided to stay. And not long after, Xingxing became pregnant with their first child. "It all happened so fast," Richard said. "And now here we are."

Four languages from birth

There may have been some uncertainty about where in the world they would live, but Richard felt no ambivalence over the language he would speak to Lada. He explained: "Here or there or anywhere, I wanted to use my own language with my own child. I just felt like I couldn't imagine talking to her in any other language. Czech is part of my whole upbringing. When I talk to her, I want to give her something of my own childhood and my own childhood is Czech. Everything is related to that; all of my childhood emotions are actually in the Czech language. Czech is me. So I wanted to share it with her, no matter what."

Czech, then, is the minority language and exposure to this language is mainly Richard's responsibility, which he has taken on with a proactive spirit. Xingxing, whose Czech is still limited, speaks to Lada in standard Mandarin. And Xingxing's mother, who lives with them, often takes care of Lada while talking to her in the Chinese dialect that Xingxing acquired as a child. Xingxing speaks with her mother in this dialect while Richard and Xingxing continue to use mostly English as their shared language. Richard also uses some Mandarin with Xingxing and a blend of both Chinese tongues when communicating with his mother-in-law, who speaks no English.

Thus, in this multilingual setting, and with additional input in Mandarin from preschool each day, Lada has been receiving exposure to these four languages from birth.

While Lada hasn't yet turned 3, Richard and Xingxing report that she is already actively using Czech with Richard and Mandarin with Xingxing. However, Richard shared a cautionary tale when he told me, "I'm pretty much with her any free time I have, and she responds to me in Czech. But this year I had a lot of concerts and I was out of the house much more often than before. So it happened that I was away for over two weeks, when before that the longest was like five days. When I came back I was really surprised because it was the first time she spoke to me in Chinese, but then she soon switched back to Czech. When she tells me something in Chinese, I keep speaking to her in Czech and then she speaks Czech again. So I'm trying to keep it strictly in Czech between us."

Music and other proactive efforts

Toward that end, Richard has sought to play the most active role he can in his daughter's young life, despite his busy professional activities. And he has come to realize, he said, that "no matter how hard and time-consuming it is," his efforts to spend substantial time with Lada are paying off in two fundamental ways: not only are his actions having a positive impact on her language development, they're also creating priceless memories and a deeper bond as parent and child.

As one example, he mentioned a recent role play game—a shopping role play—where he was the shopkeeper and Lada was the customer. As they happily engaged in this pretend play together, Richard was pleased to find that Lada could chirp away in Czech to navigate their interaction.

Xingxing added that Richard's penchant for actively playing with Lada in such ways has impressed other Chinese parents when they see the two of them together. Perhaps his efforts, then, are not only impacting his own family, this positive influence extends to other families as well.

Naturally enough, since Richard and Xingxing are both musicians, music has also been a central force in his efforts to engage Lada in Czech. "We're musicians and music is important to us," Richard said. "I play Czech songs on the piano all the time, since she was small, and it's just amazing how many songs she can remember. Chinese songs as well. She also loves to dance. She'll dance to any kind of music."

"Yeah, even when I was singing the national anthem!" Xingxing said.

"The Chinese anthem," Richard explained. "It's like a march, a fast march. We went to perform at the consulate and during the rehearsal—Lada was about a year and a half then—she ran onto the stage when we were playing the anthem and started jumping around!"

Beyond pursuing his own efforts at home to promote Czech, Richard is taking steps to connect with other Czech speakers in their area. "I made a chat group for Czech and Chinese parents and I reached out to as many people as possible. We already have almost 50 members." He said the family hopes to move to the city center in the near future, which will make it more convenient to meet Czech speakers in person.

Meanwhile, they also engage in regular video chats with his mother in the Czech Republic and make month-long visits to see Czech family and friends every summer. "Last summer I was very surprised because her Czech was even better than I thought," Richard said. "She impressed everybody by singing Czech songs and I think she was really happy that she could finally get some response because when she sings Czech songs to Chinese people, they're like, 'What's that?' But with the Czech people, they were calling out, 'Look at her! She's singing!' And she kept singing and singing to everybody. She was singing like crazy!"

At the same time, their travels in China and overseas regularly involve musical performances by Richard and Xingxing at Czech consulates and other events involving the Czech community. Such professional activities naturally reinforce the personal aim they hold for their daughter's bilingualism and bicultural identity by expanding her experience of the minority language, beyond family and friends, in stimulating ways.

Positive feelings toward the target language

For Lada, music apparently not only serves as an important source of language exposure and engagement, it nurtures her positive feelings toward the language itself. As Richard told me, in describing his outlook for all his efforts with his daughter, "I think it's important that you do it with love. I try to approach it with love and make it a nice experience for her so she has some positive emotion, it's always connected to some positive emotion."

For children in general, it's this positive emotion, this positive spirit, toward the target language that lies at the heart of sustainable and harmonious progress. Through the loving, playful efforts we make each day, we gift our children with joyful experiences that not only profoundly deepen our bond, these interactions promote a lasting passion for their minority language side and propel them forward on a productive path that can stretch a whole lifetime... and even, perhaps, reverberate long afterward in the lives of their own descendants.

AFTERWORD: In late 2020, I received an email from Richard which explained that he and Xingxing had become separated from Lada for two months because of the pandemic. In January 2020, before the outbreak of the coronavirus, he and Xingxing had traveled to the Czech Republic to record a CD, intending to stay there for only three weeks, while Lada remained in China with her family. However, Richard and Xingxing got caught up in the travel bans at that time and it wasn't until March that they were able to return to China. Richard reported that not only was this a trying experience emotionally, after their return Lada would only respond to him in Chinese. However, Richard continued to speak Czech to her and Lada gradually began communicating with him in Czech once again. Despite the initial shock he felt, Richard was evidently able to summon the patient persistence necessary to overcome this unexpected obstacle on their family's multilingual journey.

CONTACT & RESOURCES FOR RICHARD & XINGXING

- ✉ richardpohl@sina.com
- ✉ xingxingsoprano@sina.com
- 🌐 richardpohl.net
- 🌐 xingxingsoprano.com
- 🗪 WeChat ID: richardpohl
- ♪ *Magical Songs* (album of songs from the Czech Republic, China, and other countries)

3

Intentional Efforts Empower the Journey Even Before Birth

- ▶ Victor and Olya live in the U.S. state of Iowa, in a small city where the population is largely monolingual. While both have lived in the U.S. for a number of years, and speak fluent English, Victor is originally from Brazil and Olya is originally from Ukraine.

- ▶ Victor works remotely for a large language testing company, and Olya works in human resources for an insurance company. At the same time, they produce children's books and other language learning resources for families and educators through a company they founded, called Linguacious® (linguacious.net).

- ▶ They have two children: a son, Dylan, 3.5 years old, and a daughter, Isabella, 10 months. Victor speaks to the children in Portuguese, Olya speaks to them in Russian, and the couple communicates with one another mainly in English.

Victor and Olya may have grown up on opposite sides of the Earth, but their mutual love of languages ultimately brought them together somewhere in between, in a small city in the American heartland. They both had studied German and shared a mutual interest in the mechanics of German grammar.

"Our first conversation on our first date," Victor said with a smile, "we were talking about cases in German."

Olya nodded. "I wrote my dissertation about German nouns and you were working on the gender of German nouns then."

"I somehow always saw myself married to a foreigner because of my interest in languages and cultures," Victor said. "I thought that marrying somebody from my own culture and language would be a bit boring."

Two separate paths eventually cross

Victor grew up in Brazil and did his undergraduate degree in Linguistics. At the time, he had a particular interest in indigenous languages. "I thought I wanted to work with indigenous languages of the Amazon and Australia for the rest of my life. Indigenous languages make European languages look like baby talk. The grammar is so much more complicated. You have to keep track of whether something is animate or inanimate, if it's a direct object or indirect object, and this affects the form of the word, the morphology. So I was like, 'This is nice.' I like that level of difficulty."

But at his university, he recalled, he had a professor who was studying indigenous languages in the field and had the peculiar habit of scratching at himself while delivering his lectures. "At one point, I decided to ask him, 'Are you okay? Why do you scratch yourself so much?' And he's like, 'Well, every month I visit a tribe and I'm there studying their language, but I come back full of ticks.' And I'm like, yeah, maybe I'll do my Master's in something else!"

Victor went on to earn his Master's degree in Computational Linguistics from a binational program in Germany and the Netherlands. After that, he came to the U.S. to pursue his PhD in Language Learning and Assessment at a university in Iowa. It was then that Victor met Olya.

Olya's journey to the U.S. was the result of a sister city relationship between her hometown in Ukraine and the city in Iowa where she came to reside. In Ukraine, she majored in Languages and Literature and studied English, German, and Spanish. After earning her undergraduate degree, she was invited to study in Iowa and entered an MBA program.

Although Olya decided to pursue a career path that was different from the language-related professions that she had originally envisioned, like teaching or interpreting, she expressed joy at being able to revive her passion for languages in connection with the family's multilingual aim and their work creating language learning products for Linguacious. "It's really fun to bring that back because that interest has been there the whole time, just kind of sleeping a bit," she said.

Intentional efforts began before birth

Because of their longtime interest in different languages and cultures, it comes as no surprise that Victor and Olya have been very intentional about their multilingual aim for their own children. In fact, their efforts began not just at birth, but *before* birth. "We were invested in learning each other's languages," Victor said. "It was part of the courtship ritual, so to speak." Olya described the efforts she made to learn some Portuguese and Victor's efforts to learn some Russian, stressing how the language ability they gained has helped make life easier for them as a multilingual family.

The couple's proactive efforts then continued when Olya became pregnant. Intent on speaking to Dylan in their native languages after his birth, they first began doing so prior to his arrival with Victor addressing their not-yet-born son in Portuguese and Olya addressing him in Russian.

Research on the question of language input in the womb— such as the study "Language experienced *in utero* affects vowel perception after birth," led by Christine Moon and published in the journal Acta Paediatrica in 2013—indicates that pre-birth language exposure *does* have a measurable impact on the developing child. What's even more important, perhaps, is that the couple's earliest efforts to speak to their son in the two target languages enabled them to establish the new pattern of language usage that they felt suited their multilingual goal. In other words, this first step, taken before birth, no doubt helped pave the way for their routine use of these languages from the day Dylan was born, a transition that took the couple from speaking mostly English each day to a home where they consistently use Portuguese and Russian, too.

"For us," Olya said, "it was important to do this from day one and I feel like that was a very good decision. Since then I've talked to friends who tell me things like, 'I have a 4-month-old baby. I'm still speaking to him in English, but I'm going to start soon.' And that can be a difficult transition to make."

The couple's commitment to speaking the target languages extends beyond their own home as well. Victor told me, "We also agreed that we would never succumb to social pressure. Living here, there's very little multilingualism. If somebody looks at us in a weird way when they hear us speaking in other languages to our kids, we don't mind. We know we're investing in a very important goal. We're giving our kids an amazing gift."

"Sometimes, on the playground, people walk in on the situation where I'm talking to my kids in Russian," Olya said. "Initially, maybe they don't know how to react, there's some discomfort, but when I say hi and we start talking, they're okay."

"We take it as an opportunity to educate people about the benefits of bilingualism," Victor said. "The first time we meet somebody, we usually throw it out there from the very beginning: 'Hi, we talk to them in different languages, just so you know.'"

"And most will say they wish their kids were bilingual or trilingual," Olya added. "They say, 'Teach my kids,' and they're joking, but they wish that was the case."

While Victor and Olya would be happy if Dylan and Isabella eventually learn additional languages beyond these first three—Portuguese, Russian, and English—they also expressed some caution about expanding the children's exposure to other languages prematurely. Referring to Dylan, Olya said, "I wouldn't want to introduce too many languages at this point. I feel like there's a big difference between dabbling in a language and knowing a language and I think, for his age, three is plenty."

"When he turns 5, I think that's when we'll be more open to introducing a fourth language," Victor agreed. "Right now, our main goal is to really solidify the three we have at home."

Dylan, now 3 and a half, has become "very balanced in his trilingualism," Victor said. "He can talk away in all three languages."

The couple hopes that, eventually, both children will not only speak these languages well but be strongly literate in them, too.

Support from other speakers

Along with their own proactive efforts to use the two minority languages, Victor and Olya try to take full advantage of the language exposure that family and friends can provide. Their parents—particularly their mothers—have stayed with them for extended periods of time each year, with Victor's mother fortifying the children's exposure to Portuguese and Olya's mother making the same strong contribution in Russian. In fact, the six months that Olya's mother spent with the family after Isabella was born has apparently influenced Dylan's preference when it comes to communicating with his baby sister because he now uses exclusively Russian with her. "We don't know if that's going to continue," Victor said. "But it's interesting how just the amount of exposure makes a big impact."

In addition to these visits by family members, and regular online chats when they're apart, Victor was able to find a Portuguese-speaking woman to care for Isabella during the day while he and Olya are working and Dylan is attending his English-language preschool. "I'd much rather hire a Portuguese-speaking or a Russian-speaking nanny than somebody in the neighborhood just because they happen to be there," he said. "In fact, I'll pay more for that."

Beyond this caregiver for Isabella, the couple is also eager to connect locally with others who share their minority languages, inviting them, in a sense, to be a part of their family's special aim.

"Every time we meet speakers of these languages," Victor explained, "we ask them from the get-go, 'Would you please talk to them in Portuguese?' or 'Would you please talk to them in Russian? That would mean a lot to us.'"

He advised, "All you have to do is put your hands together and say, 'Can you please do me a favor? Just always talk to him in this language. That would mean so much to me.' Most people are pretty nice and are willing to comply."

Not only does some assertiveness in this way help fortify the children's language exposure, it can also provide a positive influence on their attitude toward the languages themselves by highlighting the fact that there are speakers of Portuguese and Russian beyond the smaller circle of their own family.

To date, the family hasn't yet traveled abroad, but as the children get older, they look forward to taking trips to Brazil and Ukraine to see family members and friends while immersing themselves in the language and culture of each location.

Creating resources for themselves and others

When it comes to books and other resources, Victor and Olya have mindfully emphasized their minority languages and actively sought to limit the influence of the majority language. Citing an example, Victor said, "That's one of the rules at our house: they can watch cartoons in our languages, but we never let them watch cartoons in English. It's always Russian or Portuguese— never English."

The couple has even taken up the challenge of creating their own resources after struggling to find appealing materials already on the market. Although the initial impetus for developing products was linked to the language learning needs of their own children, the couple's efforts for Linguacious, the company they founded, have expanded to include multilingual families worldwide through a growing number of products produced in a wide range of languages.

While Linguacious now offers children's picture books that include the *Little Polyglot Adventures* series (inspired by their own kids), the first product they created, a set of vocabulary flashcards with embedded audio, is designed to engage children in the target language through a variety of playful games. "I believe that if kids aren't having fun, they won't care," Victor explained. "They're not going to want to learn another language unless it's fun for them." The aim with our flashcards, he said, is to make "that first taste of the language" enjoyable and successful so that children will have positive feelings about the experience. "Because if the first experience is something they don't like, they're not going back to it. They're like, 'Yeah, I tried it and I hate it.'"

The Linguacious flashcards are now available in dozens of different languages, including endangered languages that no longer have many speakers like Irish Gaelic, Hawaiian, and the Alaskan language of Yup'ik. Victor said, "At the same time that we're trying to help families, it also works a little bit for language revitalization where we want kids to care about their languages and their heritage language—it's your culture, it's your parents' language."

Be intentional from the start

While Victor and Olya are still in the early years of their multilingual journey with their kids, their passion and talent for languages, along with the insights they've gained from fostering active trilingual ability in their young son, make their advice to new parents particularly useful to hear. Both agreed that being intentional about this aim, from the very start, is especially important for generating a positive and productive experience through the first few years.

"Yes, the keyword is intentional," Victor said. "Bilingualism won't just happen. You have to make it happen. It has to be intentional. I think having that conversation before the child arrives is crucial. That's when you still have time to think about these things, map out your resources, and make sure you have a bilingual plan. The sooner you have that plan in place, the higher your chances for success. If you're a busy parent, and on top of that you now have a baby to feed and you're waking up five times a night, you're not going to have time to map out those resources."

"Definitely start right away," Olya said. "It's much harder if you think like, 'Oh, we'll start when they reach a certain age.'"

"The other thing is for parents to model it," she continued, referring to the fact that some parents with a bilingual dream aren't consistently using the minority language themselves. "I've had friends who are speakers of the minority language and they complain about their 2 – or 3-year-old. 'He never speaks in Russian,' they say. Well, but neither do they."

"With English-speaking friends," she explained, "I still address Dylan in Russian. But I don't exclude them; I translate for them. I might say two or three sentences to Dylan and just give them a brief synopsis. I don't switch when speaking to Dylan, but I don't exclude other people, either. I always try to include them."

Any parent can produce success

Victor then offered his thoughts on the bilingual journey for parents who are native speakers, or capable non-native speakers, of the minority language, saying, "You should understand that you will be the most precious resource for your kids and a lot of the success you experience will have to do with you and your commitment. How willing are you to put in those hours, make that time for them? Because it's a matter of time, right? You want to increase the amount of input that you give them and the frequency of that input. And sometimes there are these time slots that we don't think of as time we could be giving input in the language, but actually, it is. You don't necessarily need to have a dedicated one-hour slot, right?"

Providing a personal example, he said, "I drive Dylan to day-care every day and I pick him up. It's 10 minutes to daycare and 10 minutes back. If you rode with us, you would go crazy because we talk, talk, talk, talk. It's 20 minutes of language immersion right there. I don't care what we talk about. We talk about the clouds, or the car in front of us, but it's going to be in our language. Twenty minutes every day—if you add that up, it's hours and hours of input from an early age."

At the same time, Victor shared some words of encouragement for parents who have more limited fluency in the target language. "You can still be very helpful in terms of creating an interest in the language," he said. "There are a lot of things that you can do in the house. Like when you're brushing your teeth, you can do some vocabulary learning. You can have a reward chart. Every time they learn a new word and they can use it, you can give them a star and then you have your ice cream if you get 10 stars. So there are a lot of things you can do that are fun and playful to get the kids' ears and minds open to speaking another language."

He stressed that parents in this situation, with limited proficiency, will also need to be proactive about seeking out additional support for their bilingual aim from the local community and from resources online.

Victor emphasized, too, that all parents should take full advantage of "free advice from people who have been in the same situation. With bilingualism, the more issues you're having, the more you should be talking about them with others because the easier it'll be for you to find solutions."

"So at the end of the day," he said, "whether you're a native speaker, somebody with lots of fluency, or a limited speaker of the language, there's no excuse. If the goal is clear in your mind, there is a path."

He added, "My mom always said, 'If you want to do something, there's a way. If you don't, there's an excuse.' So I think there's a bright possibility for everybody, but it's going to be easier for some and harder for others."

AFTERWORD: Victor and Olya are both so mindful and proactive about their multilingual aim for their children, in every aspect of their lifestyle that's within their control, that their thriving success is not at all a surprise. Since this interview was conducted, their daughter is following in her older brother's footsteps and becoming just as actively and confidently trilingual. The word "intentional," which Victor and Olya stressed and which other parents will also emphasize, is one of the central traits shared by every parent in this book. Put plainly, the more intentional we can be in our actions from day to day, the more success we will experience over the years of childhood. And the deep drive that both Victor and Olya feel for being intentional about their actions, in order to maximize their children's progress, essentially ensured—even before embarking on this journey with their kids—that their vision of multilingual success would be realized.

CONTACT & RESOURCES FOR VICTOR AND OLYA

- ✉ contact@linguacious.net
- 🌐 linguacious.net
- 📷 @linguacious_llc
- 🐦 @linguacious_llc
- 📖 *Little Polyglot Adventures* series (children's books available in 19 languages in both monolingual and bilingual editions)
- 📖 *The Boy Who Illustrated Happiness* (children's book)
- 🃏 Linguacious Vocabulary flashcard games

4

Non-native Family Takes Baby Steps Toward Bilingualism

▶ Elżbieta is Polish and lives in Poland. A scientist and writer, she is a fluent non-native speaker of English. She blogs in Polish about her approach to language and learning at the site Mam to na końcu języka (At the Tip of My Tongue: mamtonakoncujezyka.pl).

▶ Her husband, Michał, is Polish, too. He is also proficient in English and he works as a programmer.

▶ They have two children: a daughter, Kinga, 4.9 years old, and a son, Piotr, 3.1 years old.

▶ Elżbieta speaks to her children in English "100 percent" of the time and Michał uses English with them "around 80 to 90 percent." The couple generally communicates in English when the children are present and in Polish when they're not.

Elżbieta calls herself "a walking example of bilingualism running in the blood." Her paternal grandfather, who taught himself three languages as an adult, worked for Poland's foreign trade bureau and this brought his family to India for a stay of five years. "That's where my dad picked up really good English," she said.

When she was born, her father began speaking English to her regularly in order to cultivate her early ability in this language. "My parents are both scientists and they had the chance to travel a lot when Poland was still a socialist country. When I was around

4, we lived in England for half a year. When they were at work, I went to preschool."

Elżbieta said that, after the family returned to Poland, she was able to "hold a conversation" in English, but for the next 10 years she had few opportunities to improve her ability outside of her father's continuing efforts to use English with her and supply her with English books and other resources. At school she had to study Russian.

"Then when I was about to start middle school, my mom left for Singapore for one year. I stayed with my dad for that year, in Poland. After my mom came back, they decided that we would go to Singapore for another year because my dad found a job there, too." As it turned out, her parents extended their work for a second year, which meant that she spent two years in Singapore before returning to Poland to finish middle school and continue her studies.

The bilingual experiment begins

Elżbieta and Michał then met in high school. "We were in the same high school class," she said, "so we started dating when we were 15." Michał had attended a different primary school and, unlike Elżbieta, was able to study English at his school. In this way, his formal education became the basis for his own English ability.

After dating for a number of years, Elżbieta and Michał got married then eventually had their first child. Elzbieta acknowledged that, when she was pregnant with Kinga, she hadn't thought at all about a bilingual aim. Because bearing a child had been difficult for her, she was only focused on a healthy birth.

However, when Kinga was 6 months old, Elżbieta completed a project at the university where she was working and suddenly found herself with "loads of time." She recalled, "Then it crossed my mind that I had English-speaking colleagues at the university; I had just finished writing multiple articles in English; I read books in English; I watch movies in English. And, basically, the idea of *not* teaching her English would be like excluding her from an important part of my life."

"So that's where the idea came from," she continued. "But at first, I didn't read anything about bilingualism. I didn't even have a clue that there's something called 'intentional bilingualism.' I only had in mind that my dad did it. I knew how important the language is to my grandparents. I knew what I'd seen at work and in other countries. And all of that added together, I thought, okay, I'll see what happens if I start using English."

"It was an experiment," she added with a nod to her scientific spirit.

Her husband joins the journey

At first, Elżbieta spoke English to Kinga during the day while Michał was at work. Then, when he returned home, the family used Polish. "But my daughter was a really quick learner and she picked up Polish so quickly that I noticed this just wasn't sufficient. Even the eight hours Michał was at work didn't suffice for her to produce any English."

She then tried extending her use of English with Kinga during the weekend, too, but even so, it seemed her progress in Polish remained much stronger than her development in English.

At that point, Elżbieta sought Michał's support, asking him to use English, too. "He agreed, and he was all for it, but when it came to speaking it, he was less willing to stick to the scheme that we'd decided on. So there's still a lot of reminding and getting cross about not using the 'correct' language."

"But now," she said with a smile, "my daughter has become the policewoman because she hears me say to Michał, 'Speak English!' So she picked that up and now she tells him, 'Daddy, you need to speak English!'"

While Elżbieta said that she now speaks only English to Kinga and Piotr, she conceded that she had some difficulty with this, early on, when out in public. "At first, I was rather shy and I tended to switch back to Polish," she said. But, as time passed, she got used to sticking to English with her kids then switching to Polish with people in the community. She pointed to two factors that helped her reach this more effective use of the two languages.

"One is that we live in a neighborhood where most people have been living for the past 30 years because we live in this socialist-built high-rise. So once they got accustomed to that strange woman speaking English, it became much easier. The other is that I was frequently approached at the playground by other parents and they said things like, 'Oh, that's cool what you're doing!' or 'Do you think I could do it, too?' And I thought that, this way, I'm setting an example for others to consider doing it themselves. So it was also a matter of convincing myself and seeing that it brings value to society."

Daily efforts in and out of the home

As Elżbieta proceeded on their family's bilingual journey, she came across the expression "intentional bilingualism" and realized that this aptly described her own approach. "It means," she said, "that you introduce a language that wouldn't normally be there, that this is something deliberate. And I've been as intentional as I can be about my efforts."

While Elżbieta has been persistent about using English when her children are present, she explained that she does allow for one exception. "Books are crucial for fueling language development," she said. "I read to them in both languages because I think it's the only way I can ensure that both English and Polish reach a similar level, where my kids are using rich and varied vocabulary."

She continued, "So I decided that books should form a solid foundation for our approach. And since books for small children seem to cover a limited range of topics—things like animals, dinosaurs, space, travel—I've tried to get books on these topics in both languages. With the help of these books, not only do my kids have a chance to acquire new words, so do I."

Elżbieta emphasized the value of books in which the text rhymes. "When I read books like this to my kids, I can intentionally withhold the last word of a line and my kids will complete it with the missing word. They seem to always come away with a few more new words from our rhyming books...then multiply that by the many books we have."

"And when I read picture books to them, I ask them questions: What are the characters feeling? What will happen next? Close your eyes and name some of the things that are in the picture."

Along with books and reading, Elżbieta told me that she makes use of techniques from speech therapy: games with picture cards, jumbled up picture stories, story cubes, role play, and other activities. She became familiar with such techniques because Piotr has needed additional outside support to develop his speech. "I actively seek out as many ways as I can find for nurturing speech and language development," she said.

Elżbieta is intentional, too, about expanding the children's language input beyond the exposure she generates at home. "I'm very conscious of the fact that the more experiences I can provide for my kids, the more varied their vocabulary will be. We go to the forest to talk about plants and animals; we go to the art museum to talk about art. There's no better way of boosting language ability than taking our bilingualism for a stroll."

Her three conditions for success

To the two core conditions of exposure and need—providing ample exposure to the target language and nurturing a need for the child to use that language actively—Elżbieta said that she would add a third. "My equation is exposure, need, and positive thinking—the whole positive aura around it because this was an important thing for me. I told you that I had trouble speaking English with my kids in public, and I noticed that when I overcame that, my kids were more willing to use English. It's something that the child senses under the skin. If the parent feels uneasy about a language, then the child will assume that there's something wrong about speaking it."

I then pointed to that second condition, need. Since the children are clearly aware of their parents' ability in Polish—after all, Elżbieta is even reading to them in Polish, too—what motivates Kinga and Piotr to continue communicating in English?

"For them, I think English has become a way of bonding," she explained. "It's become our family code. Kinga started learning English when she was 6 months old, but Piotr started when he was born—even before he was born. So his first language is English. Because of that, Kinga strongly associated him with English because it's truly his first language. I suspect that when he becomes more fluent in Polish, they might try to switch to Polish when they communicate. But currently, English is their language of choice. And this helps create the strong foundation of our current situation at home."

She added that, not only have the children come to associate her with English, the fact that she has persistently emphasized this language for communication within the family has made them aware of the importance and value of English to her.

Encouraging other parents to follow this path

In October 2017, Elżbieta launched a blog to share her approach with other Polish parents who are interested in nurturing their children's ability in additional languages and enriching their knowledge of the world more broadly. Her site, called Mam to na końcu języka (At the Tip of My Tongue), focuses not only on bilingualism but on teaching a range of subject matter, including math and science, in a Montessori spirit and "in a bilingual way." To this end, she offers a wealth of ideas, with useful materials for downloading, which can help parents engage in various learning activities with their kids—whether in Polish or another language. Some of these ideas come from her experiences of other countries, enabling her to raise awareness of techniques and tools that Polish parents may not be familiar with.

Through her popular blog, and her presence on social media platforms, Elżbieta has gained a following that now seeks out her advice on the sort of "broader bilingual upbringing," as she put it, that she's pursuing with her own kids.

When I asked what some of her best advice would be for parents who dream of realizing the kind of rewarding success that she's experiencing with her children, she told me, "I would say to start with baby steps because people are really reluctant to start. They tend to put up the goal of bilingualism before them and see a huge discrepancy between what they have right now and what they want to achieve. And I always tell them: Start with the aim of introducing a tiny bit of a foreign language. I differentiate between foreign language learning and bilingualism, and I try to convince them to start with that and then you'll see that when your child picks up those first few words, you'll want more."

She added, "That's exactly the route that I've followed. I didn't start off with the goal of raising bilingual children because then I probably would have just given up."

Elżbieta mentioned that people tend to look at her family's bilingual success and conclude, too quickly, that they couldn't achieve a similar result. "They tell me, 'Oh, but you put so much time and effort into it.' And I tell them, 'I put a lot of time and effort into *writing* about it. The time I spend with my kids is the same so there's no extra work for me. The only difference is that I switched languages. I get them dressed. I take them for a walk. I build a tower of blocks. The only difference is how I talk about these things.'"

"Maybe I need to dedicate extra time to looking for good English books," she allowed. "But everything else is the work that I put into writing about how to do it and trying to convince other people to give it a try."

Returning full circle to her own family's bilingual history, she said, "It's not only language that gets handed down from generation to generation, but the love of languages as well. What's more, it doesn't take much work to get a child started on learning a language. If you're able to provide the basics of a language and bring in a range of resources to sustain that input, you and your child can then continue growing in the language together."

AFTERWORD: The idea of parents "growing in the language together" with their children is a very positive and productive way for non-native speakers of a language to view their bilingual journey. I have known many parents who are non-native speakers—in some cases, at a low level of proficiency at the start of their journey—and they have made considerable progress in their own language ability as they simultaneously seek to nurture their children's development in this language. I would also second Elżbieta's wise advice to simply begin with "baby steps" each day, instead of thinking too far ahead to the greater goal of native-like fluency. This level of fluency may gradually come, for both parent and child, but it's a dream that can only be reached by making small, persistent efforts on an ongoing basis. In the end, for any family, the journey is always composed of those baby steps, taken day after day after day, over the full length of the childhood years.

CONTACT & RESOURCES FOR ELŻBIETA

✉ ela@mamtonakoncujezyka.pl

🌐 mamtonakoncujezyka.pl

▶ youtube.com/channel/UCF05fdm7PG8pV2CN2SDtucQ

f facebook.com/mamtonakoncujezykapl

⊙ @mamtonakoncujezykapl

🌐 bilingualfuture.com (one of the creators of the Bilingual Future Project)

5

Parent Makes Success Possible with Own Language Learning

- ▶ Hossam was born in the U.S. and his first language is English. Although he had some exposure to Arabic when he was a child, he developed proficiency in this language as a young adult. An editor and translator, he has built an innovative language learning website for Arabic called The Living Arabic Project (livingarabic.com).

- ▶ His wife, Rubina, is originally from Pakistan and came to the U.S. as a child. She is bilingual in English and Urdu, and works as an electrical engineer.

- ▶ Their son, Bahar, is 5.2 years old.

- ▶ Hossam speaks Arabic with Bahar; Rubina uses Urdu with him; and, as a couple, they communicate in English.

- ▶ The family lives in Washington, D.C.

Like many people in the U.S., Hossam grew up in a household with a family member who had immigrated to this country from another nation. His father is originally from Lebanon and came to the U.S. as a young man during the time of the Lebanese Civil War. He went to college in Oklahoma and ultimately completed his PhD in Chemical Engineering at a university in Virginia.

"He met my mother in college," Hossam said, explaining that his mother is American and grew up in Michigan, where he himself was raised. Though her grandfather was from Switzerland and spoke Swiss German, "there wasn't any language passed on to my mother's generation, in terms of German or anything."

As a boy, Hossam attended a private Islamic school for eight years. While the main language at the school was English, "we also had to take Arabic classes and Quran classes and Islamic Studies classes. And those classes were so miserable because it was all grammar and rote memorization. We had to memorize passages from the Quran without even understanding what it means."

In school, he studied the written form of Arabic, commonly called Standard Arabic, which is used throughout the Arab world. However, the spoken form of Arabic varies, depending on the particular country or area, which means that there are a range of different dialects when it comes to everyday communication.

Passive ability as a child

Although his father was a native speaker of the Lebanese dialect, he generally spoke in English to Hossam and Hossam's four siblings. And because the school focused on learning to read and write in Standard Arabic, and neglected any sort of oral communication through Arabic dialects, Hossam developed some passive ability in the Lebanese dialect, but was unable to use it actively. "In other words," he said, "what we were taught in school had very little relationship to what we spoke, meaning us students who had an Arab background. I had friends of Egyptian and Syrian backgrounds, who were born in the U.S. like me, and we all had to learn the same formal language, but what is truly the native language, the spoken language, wasn't actually nurtured."

Still, the passive knowledge he gained from that time stayed with him and proved to be the seed of his later success at mastering Arabic himself and then handing down the language to his son. Recalling the summers his grandparents would visit from Lebanon, or the family would travel there, he said, "A lot of the songs and things like that ended up sticking with me in the long run."

A turning point in language learning

After graduating from high school, Hossam went to college in Michigan and majored in art. He said he loved studying art, but pointed to "a socially conscious side, especially being from a mixed background" that motivated him to join the Peace Corps after he completed his undergraduate degree. (The Peace Corps is a U.S. government program that sends skilled workers, serving as volunteers on two-year assignments, to support the needs of other nations at a grassroots level.)

Hossam's assignment took him to South Africa, where he assisted teachers and students in two local schools and sought to strengthen their programs and resources. At the same time, he became enamored with the local language, known as Xitsonga. "It was my first language learning experience after Arabic—and I had hated Arabic—but I suddenly loved learning Xitsonga because, to me, that language embodied people. When I was growing up, the Arabic I learned did not reflect people, it did not reflect fun. It was a formal, rigid language used in religion and media and political speeches, but nobody spoke it."

He continued, "So this first positive language learning experience really opened my eyes. It suddenly changed how I saw Arabic. When I came back to the U.S., I was like, 'Wow, maybe I could actually learn this if I had a better approach.'"

After returning to Michigan, Hossam took a year off to work and save money before entering graduate school. And during that year he threw himself into studying Arabic. "I went to the university bookstore and I bought all the Arabic books, and I just started doing it. I had two part-time jobs and then I would study Arabic five hours a day. I went through the equivalent of multiple semesters of Arabic on my own. The books I bought were all for the formal language because that's what 99.9% of Arabic books and textbooks and dictionaries are in. But as I studied these books, I was able to suddenly make connections to the spoken language and that passive learning I had gotten as a child, like the songs that I learned as a kid. It started to come back to me."

With this newfound passion for Arabic, Hossam then entered the Middle East Studies Department at the University of Michigan. And during a study abroad opportunity in Jordan, he met his future wife, Rubina. He explained, "She was Pakistani and studying Arabic at the same center. She was born in Pakistan, but came to the U.S. as a child—what some people call 'a generation-and-a-half immigrant' because she's not really first or second generation, she's kind of in between."

Referring to his progress in Standard Arabic, he said, "A lot of people say that they had to study a language for 10 years before they felt like they were fluent in it. But starting from when I got back from the Peace Corps to the end of graduate school—three and a half years, basically—I was at that level."

From passive to active ability

Meanwhile, Hossam also sought to improve his ability in spoken Arabic, and not only in the Lebanese dialect but in various other Arabic dialects, too. A post-graduate year in Egypt, and the work he has done in the U.S. since then, have proven fruitful for his ability in both the written and spoken forms of the language. He told me, "I came back from Egypt in 2012 and all of my jobs, from 2012 until today, have required me to use Arabic."

Among his efforts is an ongoing project that Hossam is spearheading, called The Living Arabic Project, with the goal of creating an online database of dictionaries in both Standard Arabic and in various Arabic dialects to support learners in their process of becoming proficient in both the written and spoken forms of the language. As the name of the project suggests, Hossam is seeking to create tools and techniques that will enable people to experience Arabic in a more engaging way—a more "living" way—than he did as a child.

And, naturally, his passion for this task is fueled, in particular, by his language learning aims for his son.

Teaching two forms of one language

At the age of 5, Bahar is now trilingual in English, Arabic, and Urdu. "The way it works," Hossam said, "is that I speak in Arabic—I speak a Lebanese dialect—my wife speaks in Urdu, and we both help him with English. We both grew up here so we help him when we need to, but he gets English predominantly from school, and just being with friends and other people."

Hossam and Rubina are hoping that Bahar can become literate in these three languages, too. English literacy, of course, won't be an issue, but Urdu and, especially, Arabic, will pose a sizable challenge. "Rubina grew up speaking Urdu, but she came to the U.S. when she was 4, so she wasn't literate yet," Hossam said. "Working with our son has actually been a chance for her to become literate in the language."

As for Arabic, he explained, "Essentially, I have to teach him at least two forms of Arabic: the spoken, Lebanese form and the standard written language. And like I said, linguistically, they're different enough to be called different languages. So technically, yes, I want to teach him both of these languages, but what I really want is for him to have fun with the languages and to love the languages, to love them for what they embody and what they represent."

He continued, "He speaks Arabic with me because, frankly, I'm his dad and he loves me. And he speaks Urdu with his mom because he loves his mom and he loves what she represents to him. If we start making everything into grammar lessons, he would very quickly reject those languages and he would say, 'Well, you both understand English so I'm just going to speak English to you.'"

Emphasizing books and reading

Sharing their efforts to date, Hossam began by stressing that he and Rubina interact with Bahar "exclusively" in their target languages. Her Arabic is stronger than his Urdu, though, which means that she is able to follow his interactions with their son in Arabic more readily than he can follow her interactions with him in Urdu.

Along with this proactive input through speech, Hossam also emphasizes books and reading in both languages. However, he pointed out that obtaining books in Urdu has been a much easier task. With Arabic, there are very few books written in their spoken dialect, and he has been intent on reading to Bahar in this oral variety of the language in order to nurture his speaking ability, rather than in Standard Arabic, the written form that had soured him on Arabic as a child. To overcome this lack of suitable resources, Hossam has taken English books and Standard Arabic books and translated them into the spoken dialect, printing out the text and affixing his translation to the pages. As time has passed, he has also become more adept at translating books on the fly, mentioning that he recently spun his own telling in dialect of the book *James and the Giant Peach.*

At the same time, he has also been gathering children's books in Standard Arabic to help teach Bahar this "second" form of the language. Along with books he has been able to obtain in the U.S., he said, "Whenever a friend is returning from somewhere in the Middle East, I'll ask, 'Can you bring back some kids' books for me?' Because they're all written in the standard language, I can use that to my advantage."

In this way, despite the various challenges involved in nurturing Arabic outside an Arab nation, Hossam is seeking to forge an approach that can provide an effective and enjoyable experience of both the spoken dialect and the written language.

The challenge of limited resources

While Hossam and Rubina are very pleased with the progress Bahar is making in all three languages, Hossam admits to feeling some frustration over the fact that children's resources in Arabic—and especially resources that can support his efforts to nurture their spoken dialect—have been so difficult to find compared to many other languages. "The lack of resources has really been hurting me," he said. "If there were more resources, it would be much easier. Urdu is different—it's more uniform and that makes it more straightforward—and because it's spoken not just in Pakistan but in India as well, there are way more resources for it. Honestly, for Lebanese, or even just Arabic in general—I've branched out and I've used Syrian, Palestinian, whatever—I've exhausted the resources at this point."

He then offered an example of a likely challenge in the future, saying, "One day he'll want to play video games and there just aren't any video games—zero video games—in the dialect, as far as I know, and nobody wants to play a video game in the standard language because it sounds like someone is giving a political speech. I actually reached out to a couple of people on Kickstarter. I never got a response, but I told them, 'I'll translate your game for free into Arabic.' They probably thought I was crazy, but I'd love to be able to do that, translate certain games into Arabic."

Hossam's continuing efforts in this area, where "necessity is the mother of invention," will no doubt end up producing new resources and strategies that can benefit not only his own son's ability in Arabic but also the language development of other children whose parents have chosen to nurture their Arabic. This, however, is actually another frustration that he has experienced: the substantial challenge of fostering a child's Arabic side in the U.S. often leads parents to assume that such an aim can't realistically be achieved. "I get this a lot," he said. "Parents who haven't been able to pass on the language to their kids, they feel like, 'Well, it just can't be done.' There's a defeatist attitude, I think, towards teaching Arabic, especially to third-generation kids."

Instilling a love for the language

Hossam's passion and creativity for teaching Arabic to his son, and to children in general, has prompted other families to seek out his advice for experiencing similar success. "You, as the parent, have to be very language conscious," he tells them. "You have to constantly be in a mode of observing your child to see whether they're running or they're stumbling, what their strong points and their weak points are, and you have to help them with their weak points and encourage them in their strong points. I know, for instance, that my son struggles a bit with sitting down and reading and writing so I have to find a way to encourage him by making this more fun for him."

"I also take advantage of the fact that he likes to be outside and learn about animals and plants and stuff, so it's important to look at your individual child. Keep it fun, keep it enjoyable. Don't ever make it painful for your child because that's the worst thing you could do. And that's what I worried about with my son because, last year, he was in a private school that taught formal Arabic, but it was very much like what I had gone through as a child. Here we are, and the education system hasn't actually changed that much since I was in kindergarten 30 years ago. My immediate concern was, 'This isn't going to benefit him; it's going to make him hate the language.'"

"So the most important thing," Hossam concluded, "is to instill a love for the language through having fun and through what the language embodies. I know very few people who study a language purely for its linguistic qualities. Most people, when they learn a language, they come to love the language for what it embodies because, at the end of the day, language is a form of expression of us as human beings."

AFTERWORD: Hossam's story is an inspiring example in a number of ways, starting with the fact that he was able to overcome his own shortcomings in the minority language, at an older age, through the sheer force of his conscious commitment and daily efforts. The truth is, there is no good excuse for *not* improving one's own language ability, if this aim is genuinely important to you. It simply has to be made a higher priority in your life. Of course, Hossam was still single when he was studying Arabic for five hours a day, but surely 15 minutes a day is possible for anyone. And even 15 minutes a day, if faithfully pursued, will result in significant progress over the course of months and years. I should stress, too, that Hossam's story vividly demonstrates how our own passion for a language, and for handing down that language to our children, will inevitably, in turn, touch the lives of others in ways that aid their own language learning journey. Through his work with Arabic, and through the efforts he makes with his son, Hossam is not only fulfilling his own goals, his success is also empowering the aims of other individuals and families.

CONTACT & RESOURCES FOR HOSSAM

- ✉ contact@livingarabic.com
- 🌐 livingarabic.com (access to online dictionaries)
- f facebook.com/LivingArabicProject
- 📷 @LivingArabic

6

Good Teamwork and the Key Roles Both Parents Play

- ▶ Gianluca is Italian and has lived in England for around 20 years. Fluent in English, he works as a procurement consultant.

- ▶ Alex is British and has some proficiency in Italian. She is a designer and the founder of Lil'ollo (lilollo. com), a small company that produces multilingual and multicultural products for children.

- ▶ The couple has two children: a son, Marco, 5.4 years old, and a daughter, Ornella, 3.3 years old.

- ▶ Along with English and Italian, the children are also acquiring Spanish.

- ▶ The family lives in a small city about an hour north of London.

When parents can work together as a team, with the majority language parent pitching in to lend some support to the child's development in the minority language, this empowers the family's bilingual journey in two crucial ways:

1. It makes life a little easier for the minority language parent, who may feel stressed, even overwhelmed, when it comes to promoting the target language.

2. This additional support also fortifies the process of language acquisition, enabling the child to make stronger progress.

An encouraging example of this sort of teamwork can be found in the story of Gianluca and Alex, who are each making the most of their roles as minority language parent and majority language parent, respectively. As a result, their family's experience to date has been marked by substantial success and joy.

Consistency from the minority language parent

"I think the bottom line is to be consistent," Gianluca said, emphasizing this idea throughout our conversation.

"We started right from the beginning," he explained. "We didn't start from 6 months or 9 months, as some parents do because they think, oh, there's always time. So when Marco was born, from that day I spoke to him in Italian. And with Ornella, it was exactly the same, from day one."

He went on to stress that waiting until a later stage to start using the minority language can make it more difficult to achieve a bilingual aim because the child will begin to associate the minority language parent with the language used from early on. And if that language is the majority language, shifting gears to the minority language may then become a bigger challenge, for both parent and child.

"So the most important thing is to be consistent about using your language," he said. "If I was speaking English to my kids, they would never have learned Italian. There are many older kids in the UK, and they have an Italian surname, but they don't speak much Italian. And the reason is, their parents were always speaking to them in English. Because it was easier. I even know some Italian couples in the UK—they're both Italian—and they speak with their kids in English."

Alex mentioned that the children don't often hear Gianluca speaking English because he can use Italian with her as well, when in front of the kids. In this way, the consistency he favors is further reinforced. "It helps that I have a good understanding of Italian," Alex said, "so our family conversations can be half-English and half-Italian." Thus, Gianluca can speak Italian, Alex can speak

English, and the children will switch back and forth between Italian with their father and English with their mother.

Meanwhile, when the family is with English speakers who don't understand Italian, Gianluca will use English with them but then turn to the children and use Italian. And the infrequent times he might inject a word or two of English into his Italian, when speaking with the kids, is because there isn't a good Italian equivalent for a particular English term.

The role of the majority language parent

Because of his work, where he spends the day speaking English, Gianluca said that it would probably have been easier for him to use English at home, too. However, he and Alex made a conscious decision, before their son was born, that they would employ the "One Person, One Language" (OPOL) approach and stick consistently to this use of their native languages when the children are present. (When the kids are out of earshot, the couple will generally rely on English as their common language for communication.)

At the same time that Gianluca has been steadfast about his use of the minority language, Alex, as the majority language parent, has also played a central role in the children's progress. Along with her efforts to gain ability in Italian—enabling Gianluca to avoid switching to English with her in front of the kids—she has been a proactive force for additional exposure to Italian when Gianluca is away at work. While she doesn't often speak this language directly to her kids, "There are many little ways that I'm backing up their Italian," she said.

In fact, her quest to enrich their home environment in ways that can support their multilingual aim began before the children arrived, when she was preparing Marco's nursery. "I couldn't find the kinds of bilingual products for younger kids that I wanted," she explained. "So I started designing my own bilingual language learning products for children, and maps to help children understand their family history and foster some kind of excitement in exploring the world."

Many of the appealing products that she created for Lil'ollo, the company she founded to share her work with other families, now decorate their home. Along with bilingual posters and vocabulary cards, there is a large, colorful map of the world which conveys their family's multicultural and multilingual history: beyond more immediate roots in the UK and Italy, previous generations can also be traced to the U.S., India, and China.

"I'm a very visual learner," Alex said, "and there are so many spaces and places in the home that you can use. It doesn't need to be like, 'Okay, now we're going to sit down and learn a second language.' There are many ways, as the majority language parent, that you can help enrich your environment in the minority language. Even sticking to the One Person, One Language model, you can still support the minority language."

Alex shared various other steps she takes to support the children's Italian side: writing messages in English and Italian on a large chalkboard mounted on the kitchen wall; limiting the children's TV watching and other screen time to Italian; and arranging for frequent Skype sessions with family and friends in Italy.

"And we have lots of conversations throughout the day about language," she said, explaining that she often asks the children how their father would say something in Italian or their Spanish-speaking childminder would say something in Spanish. She also mentioned playing the game "Mummy needs to learn more Italian," whereby the kids serve as her tutor (a role reversal that many children adore) and they all then benefit from engaging in these minority language moments.

"An important part of our language learning journey," Alex said, "is making sure that Italian is very present at home." She emphasized that the majority language parent needn't be fluent in the minority language, or speak it with a perfect accent, in order to support the minority language parent in "little ways" that can reinforce the child's language acquisition. And such actions on the part of the majority language parent are especially important when this parent is the main caregiver and spends more time with the children.

Other sources of language exposure

In addition to the couple's own efforts, their children have benefited from the language exposure provided by others. When the family lived in London, an Italian-speaking nanny helped with the kids.

Then, after moving to a smaller city north of London, they brought in a Spanish-speaking childminder, which has enabled Marco and Ornella to gain early ability in this language, too.

At this point, Gianluca and Alex are very pleased with the progress that both children are making, in all three languages. Alex mentioned a rewarding moment when Marco was in the living room with her, Gianluca, and Lorena, their childminder. The three adults were each using their native language to speak to him and little Marco was responding by smoothly switching from one language to the next. "It was like the United Nations!" Alex said. "It was brilliant!"

The couple acknowledged that, as the children grow older and English looms even larger in their lives, it may be harder for the two minority languages to keep pace. Still, they pointed out that their proximity to Italy and Spain is a significant advantage for their long-term aim, giving them the ongoing opportunity to immerse the kids in these languages and reinforce the efforts they will continue to make at home.

Avoiding a lost opportunity

Asked for parting words to other parents, Alex spoke from the perspective of a majority language parent by saying, "Start with your partner. Start with how much they mean to you and how much their language is an integral part of that. Make space for this essential part of them in your home. In fact, give it *more* space, *more* importance, than your language. Because if the tables were turned and your majority language was the minority language, think about how hard you would want to fight to have that be an integral part of your children's lives."

Gianluca then returned to a heartfelt theme, stressing consistency and saying, "If you don't speak to your child in your language, it's a lost opportunity that you'll probably regret in the future. And maybe someday your child will blame you for not teaching him the language that you could speak. So don't take the easy way, just using the language that's easiest for everybody. It's not easy to keep speaking your language to your kids. I'm not saying it's easy. But you have to condition yourself to do it. And when you get into the habit, it becomes easier. Then you need to keep going."

"You've always made it seem effortless," Alex said to Gianluca. "It's really good to have this conversation and to know that it actually takes a lot of persistence on your part. I think that's another thing for a majority language parent: if you have a multilingual spouse, don't take for granted that this doesn't require effort from them."

AFTERWORD: As Alex points out, the role of the minority language parent can be quite demanding, which makes the empathy and support from the majority language parent so helpful for experiencing greater success and joy on the family's bilingual journey. Even when the majority language parent lacks ability in the minority language, this parent can still consider actions that could help lighten the load of the minority language partner while advancing their bilingual aim for their kids. Gianluca's consistent efforts may serve as the main engine for the children's progress in the minority language, but, at the same time, Alex's proactive support enables that progress to proceed even more efficiently and effectively. Obviously, the actions a majority language parent might take depend on the family's particular circumstances, but it behooves every couple like this, with a majority language and minority language, to discuss the details of their teamwork and the efforts each parent could potentially make in order to maximize the success of their bilingual dream.

CONTACT & RESOURCES FOR ALEX

✉ alex@lilollo.com

🌐 lilollo.com

f facebook.com/hellolilollo

📷 @hello_lilollo

7

Non-native Parents Immerse Their Home in the Minority Language

- ▶ Cristina and Pedro live in Madrid, Spain. Their mother tongue is Spanish and they are non-native speakers of English. Cristina's English ability is very strong while Pedro's ability, though less strong, is still quite competent for daily conversation.

- ▶ Cristina is a civil servant and Pedro works in the IT industry.

- ▶ They both speak to their two children in English. Their daughter, Alicia, is 6.3 years old and their son, Daniel, is 3.3 years old.

The bilingual journey of this Spanish family is an encouraging example, in a number of ways, of non-native parents nurturing early success. It shows that, despite being non-native speakers of the target language who acknowledge shortcomings in their own language skills, Cristina and Pedro have nevertheless been able to generate significant progress in their children's bilingual ability through their attitude and actions. And even when faced with difficulties along the way, or negative views from others, their teamwork and perseverance have enabled them to overcome such obstacles, time and again, to continue advancing their bilingual aim.

And it all began, in a way, when they were teens. They met right after high school—when Cristina was 18 and Pedro was 17—and have been a couple ever since. "We've been together our whole lives," Cristina said.

Different paths to English proficiency

Though both Cristina and Pedro studied English in school, their experience of gaining active ability in this language has been different.

Cristina recalled that, back in high school, she liked French better than English. But when she began meeting people online, she "fell in love" with English and the language became a passion in her life. "I started doing everything in English because I really liked it," she said, emphasizing activities like communicating with other English speakers and watching TV programs in English. "I wasn't really studying. When you like something, when you enjoy it, you keep doing it and so you're learning. And I like that no matter how long I spend doing this, I'll never get to the point when I say, 'Oh, I know everything.' I like that—it's a commitment for life."

Meanwhile, Pedro said that his own English ability was limited until more recently. "I could pass a test, but I couldn't speak. Then, 10 or 11 years ago, we started watching TV in English with subtitles in Spanish and I started learning from the TV. Suddenly, something switched and I started speaking English with her friends when they came to visit us." Since that time, Pedro's ability has grown a lot, though he acknowledges that he isn't as focused as Cristina is when it comes to the finer points of grammar and pronunciation. "It's not so important for me," he said, "but I like it because I can communicate."

Before they had children, Cristina and Pedro traveled a lot together. Prior to Pedro's breakthrough in his own English ability, though, he would rely on Cristina during their trips abroad. "At first, I didn't speak anything with anyone," he said. "So it was like, 'You do everything. I don't want to know anything about it.'"

Cristina added, "And he would say, 'Don't leave me alone at the airport!'"

"It was a problem," Pedro admitted. "But now I'm more confident and I can understand pretty much everything. So I try to make them understand what I want and, normally, it works."

Committing to a bilingual aim

These travels, in fact, were an important source of inspiration for the couple's decision to pursue a bilingual aim with their children by raising them in English.

"I want them to have a wider view of the world," Cristina said, "not just be limited to Spain and not see anything outside it. We had that. We were able to travel to other places and see many other things."

Pedro agreed, adding, "They can go abroad and speak with other people. I think that's very important because I suffered a lot when I was in other countries and I couldn't speak because I didn't know how. It was frustrating."

Cristina recalled working at a language school in the city and knowing a teacher whose English ability was highly advanced. "She spoke English to her children and they were bilingual. I thought that was great, but I knew I wasn't at that level because everyone who met her thought she was a native speaker even though she wasn't. She knew words in English that I didn't even know in Spanish!"

She continued, "And I thought, I'd love that for our kids, but I didn't think we could do it. He was more sure than me. He was like, 'Yeah, you can do it!' And I was like, 'No, I don't know English well enough.' But then I looked into it online and I read some books and everything said that even if your English isn't that good, you can still do it. And I said, 'Well, if we got here from zero, they'll go farther than we did.' So we decided to go for it. And then Pedro said, 'Well, if you do it, I'll do it, too!'"

"I was thinking that only Cristina could do it," Pedro said, "but in the end, I thought, why not? I can try and, well, my English isn't perfect, but it's better than nothing."

"I was concerned because I was thinking he makes a lot of mistakes," Cristina said. "But then I thought, I make mistakes, too, but any mistakes will be corrected over time." She also mentioned hearing from some people that providing more language exposure, even if the quality of that input was lower, would be more effective than a lesser amount of exposure of higher quality. "I think they were right. It worked. The kids made mistakes, things that Pedro would say, but they corrected them over time."

While Cristina and Pedro naturally hope that their children's English ability will grow as strong as possible, they also hold healthy expectations about their bilingual aim. "We want them to speak English as well as they can," said Cristina. "Not perfect, because we think that's impossible given that we don't speak it perfectly, either. But hopefully, better than us so they don't have to struggle like we did when we wanted to improve our English."

Making a range of proactive efforts

Before Alicia was born, the couple made proactive efforts to prepare themselves and their home for her arrival. "I was trying to learn nursery rhymes," Cristina said. "And we were getting everything in English that we could. We spoke only English to her from day one and we decided that nothing at home could be in Spanish. We didn't allow any Spanish-speaking toys, Spanish books, Spanish media. And if we got a Spanish toy or book from someone, we would give it to my parents so that we still had it, but it wasn't in our home."

Along with the English exposure provided daily by Cristina and Pedro, Alicia also received some additional input in this language from Cristina's father and an American babysitter. And when Daniel was born, because Cristina was then suffering from tendinitis and couldn't hold the new baby, they brought in an American woman who helped with the children—and spoke English to them—on a roughly full-time basis for that first year.

Since then, they have continued with weekly home visits from English-speaking babysitters and, in July—when the children are out of school but Cristina and Pedro are working—they have an English-speaking nanny watch over the kids each day for seven hours.

Meanwhile, as Alicia and Daniel have gotten a bit older, Cristina and Pedro have also sought to connect with other English-speaking families in the area so their children can engage in English with other kids. Cristina explained that a trip they took to England, when Alicia was 4 and Daniel was 1, underscored for her the importance of creating opportunities for more interaction with children, beyond the substantial amount of time they're already spending with adults. "When we went to England, I loved that Alicia could play with other children and learn that kind of vocabulary," she said. "It's completely different from the way we speak."

At this point, the family is involved in the activities of three local English-speaking groups: one where the families get together monthly to do activities together in English, like reading books and making crafts; a second that involves monthly outings like bowling and ice skating, carried out in English; and a third, a smaller group of four families, where they try to meet as regularly as possible, at their homes, so the kids can play together in English.

On top of the productive efforts they're making in Spain, Cristina and Pedro have continued to view travel as a priority. After their first trip to England as a family, they returned the next summer for a second visit, when Alicia was 5 and Daniel was 2, and they hope to make many more trips together in the future so the kids can be immersed in an English environment and have the chance to play with native-speaking children. Explaining their thinking behind this aspect of their bilingual journey, Cristina said, "We wanted them to see that English was spoken outside Spain, that it was spoken not only by us and some random adults, but that there were also places where English was used by everyone and that it was useful."

Emphasizing English resources

Cristina and Pedro have also been very proactive about the resources they have at home to promote their target language. While the early restriction on Spanish books and other materials has been loosened somewhat, because Alicia is now reading in Spanish, too, and doing homework for school, they continue to emphasize English resources far more strongly.

"We have a lot of books," Cristina said. "I try not to buy too many, because we don't have room on our bookshelves, but there are always some that I want. Pedro told me, 'We're not buying anymore.'"

"We don't have any more space," Pedro said.

"Yeah, but we can give away the older ones," Cristina replied. "And the ones that were for Alicia are for Daniel now. Alicia needs bigger books, more challenging ones."

The problem of "too many books" is faced by many families, though this is a far better problem than the problem of not having *enough* books in the target language. Still, it's an ongoing challenge since, as children grow and mature, they *need* new books that will match their evolving language level and personal interests. One possibility, of course, is the use of digital books and an e-reader of some kind, but many parents aren't very keen on this option, particularly for younger kids. As Cristina told me, "I don't want them to have any more screen time. I'd rather they have physical books."

Movies, on the other hand, needn't take up much shelf space these days. "We have a hard drive with a million movies," Pedro said. "They can watch whatever they want, but only in English."

"On Fridays, we have movie night," Cristina said.

"It's movie night with pizza," Pedro added. "They like that a lot."

"Yes, and they get lollies. They get sweets. You know, children are always asking for sweets and this way, if they ask us, we can tell them, 'Sorry, it's not Friday.'"

Cristina continued, "And all the TV shows that they like, we get them online. We could watch real TV if we want, but the commercials are still in Spanish. And if they're watching TV, we want them to be watching everything in English."

"For us, it's also better watching TV shows like this because we can control the time," Pedro said. "There's a little problem, though. Because they don't watch commercials, they don't know what they want for Christmas!"

"Sometimes, if their friends have something, they know what they want," Cristina said. "But they never say, 'Oh, I want that for Christmas because I saw it on TV!'"

Satisfying both exposure and need

It's clear, then, that Cristina and Pedro have been very effective in fulfilling the first "core condition" for bilingual success: providing their children with ample exposure in the target language. At the same time, they also have been able to satisfy the second "core condition"—getting their children to feel the need to use this language actively—despite the fact that they themselves are native Spanish speakers and have continued to regularly use Spanish as their shared language as a couple, even around the kids at times. How?

Cristina explained: "When Alicia was 2, there were two words she would only say in Spanish, 'yes' and 'water'; she wouldn't say these words in English. Our babysitter was American and one day she was able to get Alicia to say 'water' in English, which we couldn't get her to say because she knew that when she asked for water in Spanish, she still got water even though we told her, 'No, you have to say 'water' in English.' But she wouldn't say it. The babysitter, though, wasn't supposed to speak Spanish with Alicia so she pretended not to understand her. And so Alicia started saying 'water' in English. Then we realized that because we showed we understood the word in Spanish, she was continuing to say it in Spanish. After that, we said, 'Wow, this is what we have to do. We can't show that we understand.' And with small children, a lot of times you really *don't* understand them. So they saw that when they spoke English, they were understood most of the time, but when they spoke Spanish, they weren't. So in the end, they started using English words instead of Spanish ones."

It seems that once English took root in this way, the emotional bond that developed between parent and child became tied to this language. This deeply ingrained bond then enabled the family to sustain English as their common language to this point—even though the children are now obviously aware that their parents speak Spanish, too.

When I asked their reaction to how non-native parents are sometimes perceived for not using their native language with their children—that "they can't communicate at a deeper level with their own children because they're not using their mother tongue"—Cristina responded in this way: "I hear people say that you can't really love them in the same way, but this makes no sense to me because feelings are feelings, they have no language. Saying 'I love you' or 'Te quiero' is the same thing. There's no difference. What I'm feeling is exactly the same thing, I'm just saying it in one language or another."

She went on, "It's true that you can't say things exactly the way you want to say them, but you get as close as you can and they're not missing anything, really. In fact, I remember one time at school, they had to draw their family and write something. Most children wrote things like 'My family' or 'My beautiful family' or 'I love my family.' But Alicia wrote, 'My family loves me.' So she knew, as well as the other children, or even better, how much she was loved."

Meeting difficulties with patient persistence

While the family has certainly experienced a lot of success on their bilingual journey together, it's also true that there was some early concern over Alicia's language development in Spanish. Although she began going to nursery school when she was one, and was immersed in Spanish each day, by the age of 3 she was still well behind her Spanish-speaking peers.

"It was hard," Cristina said, "but I read about other people who went through this and they all managed. When something happened at school, she wasn't able to tell the teacher. She just cried. That was her way of communicating. She was behaving more like a younger child instead of like an older one so she wasn't really suffering that much. It was just frustrating for her at those times. She told us she liked the school. It was true that she was having trouble communicating, but she still liked it. She was happy there."

Cristina admits being worried about Alicia's early development in Spanish and wondered whether there was some kind of speech problem affecting her language acquisition. But a speech therapist reassured her, pointing to the gradual progress Alicia was continuing to make.

Pedro noted that Alicia was always an independent child and was content playing by herself, which meant, in those early years, that she wasn't often stretching her Spanish through interactions with other kids.

"I think children are very practical," Cristina said. "Do I need this language? If so, I'll make the effort. But if I can get by without it, why bother? It's okay to speak just one language."

Along with this point about a child's pragmatic nature when it comes to communication, Cristina also stressed that *time itself* is central to a child's bilingual development. "If you don't have as much exposure as everyone else, you can't be at their level, at least until you're older. My children are going to need more time because they haven't had enough time yet. Part of it is maturity, but part of it is time, I think."

"It can be hard," Cristina said, referring to the bilingual journey. "But if you want to do it, don't give up. Keep going."

"And don't be afraid," Pedro added. "You will be fine. And in the end, it will be worth it."

AFTERWORD: Since our interview took place, Cristina told me that Pedro has begun using Spanish with the children, in order to help strengthen their Spanish side. Though Alicia and Daniel are now progressing well in Spanish, too, she said she wonders if she and Pedro "overdid it," early on, in promoting English to the exclusion of Spanish. Of course, different viewpoints on the challenge of nurturing two languages simultaneously can both be valid—so much depends on the particular circumstances of the family involved—but, generally speaking, it's "easier" to help the majority language catch up to the level of the minority language than it is to do the opposite. With Alicia and Daniel, it may be true that if more emphasis had been placed on Spanish from the beginning of their bilingual acquisition, this could have undercut the strong progress they were able to make in English. We can't actually know what might have happened if that had been the case, but in other families, it's clear that an early imbalance of exposure toward the majority language often hinders the child's development and use of the minority language, with the majority language growing overly dominant. So there's no "right" answer to this question of balance between the two languages, and that answer, as well, will likely evolve over the years of childhood, depending on the child's needs. But I suggest that it's wise to err on the side of caution, especially during the first few formative years, and, if possible, give the minority language a strong head start. Once the child has a firm and active foundation in the minority language, more efforts can be made to support the child's majority language, as needed.

8

Persistence Drives Development of a Less Common Language

- ▶ Undraa is originally from Mongolia and has lived in Denmark for 15 years. She speaks Mongolian and is also proficient in English and Danish. She works in project management.

- ▶ Her husband, Benjamin, is Danish. Along with his mother tongue, he is fluent in English and is actively learning Mongolian. He is a lawyer at the Danish Labor Union.

- ▶ They have two sons: Arslan is 6 years old and Tamir is 3.5 years old.

- ▶ Undraa speaks to the children in Mongolian, Benjamin speaks to them in Danish, and the couple communicates with each other mainly in English.

- ▶ The family lives in Copenhagen.

Growing up in Mongolia, Undraa encountered other languages at an early age. She was introduced to Russian at her elementary school while her father began teaching her English. "I was always good at languages," she said. "I had a tendency to learn fast and to pronounce things correctly. So when it's like that, it's easy to learn and I get curious about different languages."

In college, she majored in Journalism and English Translation. After graduating from her university in Mongolia, she came to Denmark to study Economics and Business Administration in a graduate program. "Luckily, it was an English program," she said, acknowledging that she had no ability in Danish when she arrived in the country. "Everything was in English. Then a few years later, I decided to go to Danish classes and start learning it. That was a whole different thing because I was older and it was harder. I realized that the older you get, the harder it gets."

After 15 years in Denmark, Undraa has gained strong ability in Danish, yet, for her, "it's still a third language" after Mongolian and English. She mentioned not feeling fully confident in this ability when it comes to humor and other nuances of the language.

Meanwhile, Benjamin studied English and German while in school, and is now quite fluent in English, though he said he's less confident when it comes to German. Currently, he's making diligent efforts to learn Mongolian, seeking to have this be "a fully functioning language in our family." He nodded to Undraa and said, "It's really hard so I can totally agree with the fact that the older you get, the harder it is to learn a new language."

Behind their multilingual aim

Undraa and Benjamin are both intent on having their children become proficient in Danish and Mongolian—and then English as well—from a young age.

"Naturally, Danish comes very easily to them because this is where we live," Benjamin said. "But I think it's really important for the relationship between the children and Undraa that their level of Mongolian will be very good, too, so that they can have advanced conversations and exchange feelings and emotions. And I want to be part of that because I'm part of the family as well. So that's my ultimate goal. I'm sure that they're going to be good in Mongolian. I just want to make sure that I'm not totally on the side of everything; I want to be part of it all."

Undraa pointed to a similar motivation, at the deeper level of the heart, when it comes to her aim to hand down Mongolian to her sons. "For me, it's very personal," she said. "I had this feeling that if I get older here, I would be very lonely if I couldn't speak with my children in my own language. So, in that sense, I really wanted them to be able to know me as who I am. That's the aim, basically. And that's why it's always a priority for me because it's very personal."

While English is another important language for the family—it's the main language that Undraa and Benjamin use to communicate with one another, though they also use some Danish and some Mongolian, too—their circumstances make it far easier for the children to acquire English compared to a less common language like Mongolian.

"I don't worry about English," Undraa said. "English is a very big language, especially here in Denmark. It's taught from very early in the schools and almost everybody speaks English fluently. And when you come into the working environment, it's almost a requirement that you speak English."

"Yeah, we're not teaching them at all," Benjamin agreed, "and they're still picking it up from TV and, of course, from us speaking English to each other. Actually, it's more important to try to keep them a little bit away from that, because we don't want English to overwhelm their Mongolian. We have a hard enough time trying to make sure that Mongolian is around them."

Language use within the family

When Undraa and Benjamin first met, she didn't speak Danish, and he didn't speak Mongolian, so naturally they used English to communicate. Then, to aid Undraa's acquisition, they began speaking more Danish together. But as soon as they had kids, they returned to emphasizing English as their shared language so that Undraa could minimize her use of Danish at home. At the same time, they remained very consistent about speaking their own native language with the children.

I asked Undraa if she ever feels shy or awkward about speaking Mongolian to her kids in public, as such feelings aren't uncommon among parents of the minority language when out in the community. "That feeling is always there," she admitted. "I always feel awkward when I speak my own language because I notice people looking at me when I speak. I'm not speaking English or German. It's totally something that they haven't heard before. Some people give me a look—probably not negative, but just 'what was that?'—then I become very self-conscious. But I still keep in mind that I need to keep at it. So I always try to speak Mongolian to them, even in public."

As siblings in Denmark, Arslan and Tamir tend to use Danish to communicate. "I tried many ways to get them to speak Mongolian to each other, but it just didn't work," Undraa said. "I sometimes tell Arslan to speak Mongolian with Tamir, and he will, but after some time, it just goes back to Danish."

However, the boys' use of the two languages also depends on the situation or setting, the *context* of their communication. Benjamin explained, "I've noticed that when we're in Mongolia, especially after the first week, it's like their Mongolian comes out of nowhere. They start talking to each other more in Mongolian."

"I think it depends on the surroundings," Undraa said. "When they're in fully Mongolian surroundings, they speak Mongolian."

"I've even heard Arslan dreaming in Mongolian," Benjamin added, "because sometimes he speaks when he's dreaming. So the Mongolian is there, right under the surface."

Obtaining resources for a less common language

Families supporting less common languages, like Mongolian, are often faced with challenges involving fewer and harder-to-get resources along with less access to a community of families with a similar language learning aim.

"The number one difficulty," Undraa said, "is that there are no Mongolian resources in Denmark. I try to seek out different resources when we travel, or online, but it really takes a lot of research. On top of that, the resources need to change all the time because the kids are growing and their interests are changing."

"Plus," she continued, "there aren't that many Mongolians living here in Denmark so I can't really ask for help. And even if I did, they have the same challenge as I do!"

"Every time we go to Mongolia," Benjamin said, "Undraa buys a lot of books, like 50 books. I have to weigh our luggage very carefully!"

Although they've been able to build up a sizable home library of books in Mongolian, finding other kinds of engaging content—like DVDs with animated movies—has been even more difficult. "There's so much focus in Mongolia on learning English," Undraa explained. "Everybody wants to or needs to learn English. I bought some DVDs, and when we watched them, they were all in English, not Mongolian."

Despite these frustrations, advances in modern technology are also aiding their ongoing efforts to bring Mongolian resources into their home. One beneficial new service is a package of TV channels from Mongolia that they are now able to access with a special device attached to their TV.

Early efforts eventually produce progress

When Arslan was born, Undraa began speaking to him in Mongolian while wondering what more she could do to ensure that he would speak Mongolian, too, when he was older. Through the research she did, she realized how important it was to provide ample input in the target language through the first few formative years, including a regular routine of reading aloud from as early as possible. "I started doing a lot of small things," she said. "I was trying to be more verbal. To be honest, I'm not a very talkative person, so that was a challenge. I was reading books. I started seeking out other Mongolian mothers and meeting up with them. I had regular conversations on Skype with my parents."

"Until he was three," she continued, "I couldn't really see much progress. But after that, he really started speaking and he got into books. He was obsessed with books and comic books and wanting to read out loud. We also traveled back to Mongolia. And during that trip, things got even better and he started speaking with my parents."

After achieving this early success with her firstborn, Undraa acknowledged feeling more "distracted" after her second son was born and, without realizing it, perhaps "neglected" to carry out her efforts as intently. It's also true, she said, that the boys have different personalities and Tamir is a less verbal child than Arslan.

At this point, at ages 6 and 3, she described their ability in Mongolian by saying, "Arslan speaks mostly Mongolian to me, but when he's eager to tell me about something, he might switch to Danish. Tamir feels more comfortable in Danish, I think. But I always remind him to switch to Mongolian, and if he doesn't, then I ask him to repeat after me and he repeats it. He understands everything, and when we go to Mongolia, he'll speak it. But still, compared to his brother at that age, he's behind."

Support from the majority language parent

In families like this one, where the majority language parent has little or no background in the minority language, the job of nurturing that language must understandably be shouldered by the minority language parent. However, unlike many such families, Benjamin is making a keen effort to learn the minority language and engage with the minority language culture. Aiming to grow as fluent as possible so that his ability can benefit both himself and his family, he studies Mongolian on a daily basis and has a weekly Skype lesson with a teacher. "It's hard to learn Mongolian when I'm not in Mongolia," he said. "But I don't feel like I have any sort of excuse not to do it. Undraa has learned Danish. So I kind of feel like I owe this to her."

Benjamin explained that, while he doesn't think his learning Mongolian can ever really be of direct support to his kids, it can still impact them and Undraa's family—as well as his own life and career—in positive ways. For the boys, he believes that his example of showing interest in Mongolian, and demonstrating his diligence toward learning it, can also encourage them in their own bilingual journey. And with regard to Undraa's family, "I want to be able to speak with them. Her mother doesn't speak English. So when we communicate, it's sign language and a lot of smiling. Her brother, too, doesn't speak English well. So something's lacking there."

Immersion experiences in Mongolia

Along with the persistent efforts being made in Denmark to nurture the children's Mongolian side, Undraa and Benjamin have also been committed to traveling back to Mongolia each summer, for three or four weeks, to meet her family and immerse the boys in the language and culture. Not only have these trips had a powerful impact on their language development and cultural identity, Undraa said that these experiences have also helped fortify her own spirit, enabling her to feel more confident about their progress. Referring to the struggles of her journey, she explained, "There's always some sort of—maybe guilt is too strong a word—that I'm not doing enough. 'I could have done this better. He still has an accent. He doesn't understand this word. He didn't remember this.' I have that all the time. But especially when we're back in Mongolia, and they're using the language, I get a lot of praise from people and, of course, that gives me a very big boost."

What Undraa is describing—the *psychological* challenge of raising a bilingual child—is quite common among parents on a bilingual path. Intellectually, we may recognize that we don't have to do this perfectly in order to realize significant success. Emotionally, however, the dissatisfactions with our efforts or our children's progress can give rise to doubts and concerns that undermine both our momentum and our joy of the experience itself. When we're drawn to our dissatisfactions, the positive side of the coin is that such dissatisfactions can potentially motivate us to undertake more effective actions. The negative side, though, could eventually be keen discouragement that threatens the entire journey itself. To sustain our quest, and soldier past the inevitable dissatisfactions of the process, we must also consciously emphasize the *satisfactions* of our experience.

Thus, these rewarding times in Mongolia have served to empower Undraa with the confidence to carry on, knowing that the satisfactions of her journey can continue to outweigh the dissatisfactions she may still feel. Moreover, the success of their yearly trips has persuaded both Undraa and Benjamin that the chance to spend more time there—even moving there for a year or longer—could benefit the whole family in important ways.

"This is partly because I've lived in Denmark a long time already—15 years—and now it's time to get closer to my parents," Undraa said. "And I want my parents and my kids to have a closer relationship, too. I'd also like them to be part of the culture because I hear from some parents with older children that even though they speak the language, when they become teenagers, they don't want to go back there anymore. I don't want that. I want them to develop some sort of fondness towards Mongolia. They don't necessarily have to live there, but they still have a connection, a bond."

Of course, a move to Mongolia would create the opposite challenge for their bilingual aim: Mongolian would become the majority language and Danish would be the minority language. "As part of my own language development," Benjamin said, "I would want to try using Mongolian in the family for a while. But then, as I'm sure would happen, their level of Danish would start to slip and I would have to switch to speaking Danish to them and keep it up by calling my parents and making visits to Denmark. So the change would be 180 degrees. But I don't think it would be as hard for me as it is for Undraa. They already have the foundation in Danish so I'm not worried about that."

Keep riding this rollercoaster

While the bilingual journey can be a challenging quest for any minority language parent, those supporting a less common language, like Mongolian, may find this aim even more demanding. After she described her experience as "a rollercoaster," I asked Undraa how she was able to overcome the tougher moments. She told me, "The number one thing is, I go to the forum [The Bilingual Zoo]. There are so many different parents giving support to each other, cheering for each other. So when I'm feeling frustrated, I go there and it gives me a big boost. And number two is my husband. He's a very involved father and he supports me 100%. It's mainly because he understands me, what's important to me, but also, he really wants to be part of my children's journey."

"I think the reason I put effort and support into it," Benjamin said, "is because I just couldn't imagine myself *not* doing it. It's our future together. She's important to me and her background is important to me. It's something I would never want to hide or put under the covers. It has to come out and they have to be proud of their mother and the Mongolian language, culture, and history. I mean, this is our family. It can be hard, but it's also extremely rewarding."

Undraa then stressed how vital it is to believe in the importance of your own language—even "small languages"—when others may question that importance. "A lot of people think Mongolian isn't an important language," she said. "It's not going to be used anywhere but Mongolia. So why would you do it? Why is it so important? So if you're going on this journey, those are doubts you shouldn't have. Mongolian is a language, too, and it's also personal to me. It's my identity. Just like someone else feels about speaking their own language, it's the same for me even though it's a small language."

Despite the longer odds of success, Undraa and Benjamin have been able to nurture significant progress toward their bilingual aim. "In the beginning," Benjamin said, "the key is persistence and keeping at it. It's so easy to give up when you don't see any progress, no real evidence that it's working, because you're just talking to a little person who can't really respond yet. There were times when Undraa felt frustrated. 'Should I drop this?' But she never really intended to. She was just saying this as a way of getting those frustrations out."

"That's the most important thing," Undraa agreed. "You keep going. You never give up. Whatever you're doing—speaking to them, reading to them—you keep going. Even though they're not speaking to you, even though you're not seeing results, you just keep going."

AFTERWORD: Undraa mentioned to me that she hesitates when it comes to telling people about her deeper motive for handing down Mongolian to her children. She said that others often misconstrue the idea of this aim being "personal" to her, that somehow this means she's prioritizing her own needs above her children's needs. For many minority language parents, though—including both Undraa and myself—our deepest motivation is inevitably "personal" because we want our children to know us at the most soulful level possible and this is intrinsically tied to our native language and culture. In this sense, our bilingual aim does serve our own needs, but it simultaneously also serves the needs of our children because it enables them to inherit half of their rightful identity and experience a much richer bond with us as their parents. To Undraa, handing down her native language and culture to her kids, to the extent she can, is her "duty" and "perhaps the only gift I can really give to them." Moreover, as she stressed to me, it's actually this personal, heartfelt reason which empowers the whole, lengthy journey, even through the tougher times. "Every time you want to quit," she said, "you remember this reason, which is so strong in your bones that it outweighs the difficulties you're facing at the time. This, to me, is the secret ingredient for perseverance."

The Primary School Years

The second stage of the bilingual journey covers roughly the years of primary school. When children begin their formal schooling in the majority language, this experience of daily immersion brings a significant shift in the balance of exposure between the two languages. Prior to this time, parents are generally able to spend more time with the child, and provide more input in the minority language. So the challenge of this second stage involves maintaining as much exposure to the minority language as possible, while sustaining the child's active communication. Advancing literacy in this language is also often an important aim for many families.

9

Early Discouragement Is Transformed into Trilingual Success

- ▶ Amy is French, but spent much of her youth in Spain and attended a British school there. She speaks French, Spanish, and English and works in the international division of an insurance broker. She is also an active blogger at "Our ml home" (ourmlhome. wordpress.com).

- ▶ Her husband, Juan, is Spanish and is trilingual in the same three languages. He works in the financial department of a French company.

- ▶ They have two daughters: Julia, 7.2 years old, and Elsa, 3.6 years old.

- ▶ The family lives in Paris, where their majority language is French and their minority languages are Spanish and English.

Considering the success Amy is now enjoying with her two trilingual daughters, and her influential presence online as a generous source of support for other parents, it's hard to believe that her own multilingual aim was nearly abandoned early on in her journey.

"I was this close to giving up," Amy admitted.

Amy was born in France, but when she was 9, the family took a trip to Spain and her father was smitten. He decided that the family would leave France behind and start a new life in Spain.

"My dad had the chance to put me in a British school there," she said. "He thought, well, if I put my French daughter in an English school in Spain, she'll master the three languages quickly and she'll be trilingual."

When she turned 18, Amy then continued her studies in England, where she lived for the next six years. Although she had hoped to return to Spain, the country was struggling economically at the time and so she went back to France.

"It was my home country, but I didn't really know it that well," she said. "I was 24 and I discovered a lot of things that, culturally, I didn't really realize before, even though my parents had raised me in French. We were a minority-language-at-home family."

Early discouragement with their multilingual aim

Though Amy grew up as a trilingual child, she initially felt that three languages would be "too much" to introduce to her own children, that, at least in the beginning, the focus should be limited to French and Spanish. But when she was expecting Julia, their firstborn, Juan suggested that they include English, too, which persuaded Amy to pursue all three languages simultaneously.

"We have very arrogant aims," she said with a laugh. "We want them to be trilingual and triliterate in French, Spanish, and English. And in a balanced way, to put the stakes even higher."

Yet the discouraging results of their first four years on this multilingual journey nearly derailed their dream.

Amy explained, "Our strategy was, originally, English for me, Spanish for Juan, and French as a family. But that was a mistake, and I only found out after, unfortunately." She said they were actively using all three languages with Julia because they wanted "a balanced trilingualism and we thought it would be a nice way to do it. We didn't want to exclude French. I mean, I'm French, and the community is French. So at the dinner table, if we were discussing something together, it would be in French. However, if I said to my daughter, 'Darling, go and get me a fork,' I would say it in English."

"But at the time," she continued, "I hadn't read anything on raising trilingual kids. I was raised as a trilingual kid and I didn't expect to have a child who would resist the minority languages."

As Julia became more verbal, she relied largely on French to communicate with Amy and Juan. "She spoke French most of the time," Amy said. "Juan had a bit more success with Spanish, but she hardly ever replied in English. And then she started schooling in French when she was 3 and it was even worse after that. She knew I spoke French so, you know, why bother?"

Recalling that time, Amy sighed. "She said it clearly one day when I asked her why she didn't speak much Spanish and English. She said, 'But French is easier.'"

The turning point on their journey

The turning point came with the birth of Elsa, their younger daughter, when Julia was 3 and a half. Amy realized that their original approach would have to change.

"I thought, this is not going to work. If the eldest speaks in French, then the youngest is going to follow. We have to do something. So that's when I started reading a lot more about this."

As she read about other parents' experiences, she came upon a father with a similar problem and the potential solution hit her: "French has got to be out. It's just killing off everything else."

"I obviously didn't want to change everything all in one go," she said. "After I read that, I thought, 'I should try and not speak French.' And since Juan speaks English, that's not a problem for us. We both speak the same languages. So one day I started speaking English from dawn to dusk, never French. Even with Juan, I addressed him in English. And by the end of that day, my eldest started trying to string together a few words in English. I was like, 'Oh, that's it! That's it!' It was priceless. When she started saying these words, my husband was there and we looked at each other and we just knew. 'French is out,' I said. And he said, 'Yeah, French is out.'"

Limiting the influence of the majority language

Amy refers to this pivotal shift in their efforts as "kicking French out of our home," a description that she admits can sound shocking to some. "Some people feel insulted," she said, "but it's nothing against my mother tongue. I love it. It's a beautiful language. But this is to protect the other languages and help my daughters learn them. It's not because I hate French."

In other words, Amy recognized that, in order to experience more success at their trilingual aim, they needed to be more intentional about emphasizing Spanish and English. This meant "de-emphasizing" French and limiting its influence, at least until the children had made more progress in the minority languages and had grown to use them more actively.

"Otherwise, kids take the easy way out," she said. "That's what I've learned with my eldest. You know, why bother using cutlery when I can use my hands? Why walk when Daddy can carry me? Kids are like that. They're pragmatic. It was the same logic for my eldest. 'Oh, French is easier.' So then what do you do? We had to push her a bit to take the hard way for her own good."

Once Amy and Juan made the decision to "kick French out of their home," they went about this in a wide range of proactive ways. Starting with their own language use, they no longer spoke French to their children; instead, Amy spoke only English and Juan spoke only Spanish, whether with the girls or with each other. (Amy has since begun using some Spanish, too, to fortify the input in this language, but continues to avoid speaking French within the family.)

To help Julia maintain this new use of languages, Amy gave her "a secret golden envelope" and "a mission": take the contents of the envelope—three small printed flags—and stick them on the front door. The Spanish and British flags went on the outside of the door to signal that Spanish and English should be used inside the house, not French; and the French flag went on the inside of the door to convey that French could again be used when you stepped outside. In this playful way, Amy sought "to help her understand that we were changing the rules of the game."

At the same time, Amy was determined to promote exposure to the minority languages, and limit the influence of the majority language, by being as intentional as she could about the resources in their home. She set about substituting French resources with resources in Spanish and English, and has been so successful in virtually eliminating French from their home that, she said with a laugh, "Our house is now like a Spanglish Embassy!"

In fact, their experience of the first four years has led Amy to be very mindful, very careful, when it comes to French. "Everything can be a trigger for switching languages. Switching itself isn't a problem, it's good, but obviously I'm trying to have them switch to the minority languages, not to the majority language." She then offered an example, explaining why she turned around all the French books on their bookshelves to hide the spines. "My eldest wasn't reading yet, but I knew it would happen. And I thought, if her gaze lands on a French book, she might switch. I do it myself, so why wouldn't she?"

Amy admits that some of her friends think she's "completely crazy" but she now believes that the success she seeks requires her to be as mindful and proactive as possible. "It won't happen on its own," she said. "I thought—stupidly, naively—that it would happen because I myself went to a bilingual school where all the kids accepted being bilingual or multilingual. I didn't realize that my context, my setting, was different and it won't happen as easily. I have to influence it."

While Amy and Juan had to be firm in their efforts to encourage Julia to use the minority languages, they also recognized that they had to be patient. "When we changed our approach," Amy recalled, "it was the beginning of August and by Christmas she was almost not using any French. When we started without French, we had to be tolerant because she was struggling so we let her use French words, but she would put in the English words or the Spanish words where she could. And over those six months, roughly, she used less and less French as she picked up more English and more Spanish."

Success is just another attempt away

Along with the many efforts made at home to nurture the minority languages, which have also included childminders with proficiency in English or Spanish, regular trips to Spain to see extended family and friends have also had an important impact on the children's Spanish side. (The girls have not yet traveled to an English-speaking country, but Amy looks forward to taking them to England in the future.)

Looking back on a particularly memorable trip to Spain, which took place after they were well into their new approach, Amy said, "The Christmas after we started implementing no French at home, we went to Spain and I could tell that my in-laws were very emotional because they were at last able to have a conversation with Julia. And that really touched me. It was like, wow, this is starting to work. It was so rewarding after four years of hardly seeing any progress. That was really important for us as a family."

Through her experience, Amy has come to realize that success awaits on the other side of what seems like failure. But to get there, you have to rise above your discouragement and make another proactive attempt. And the truth is, there are *always* more attempts available to you, which means that every failure can potentially become the springboard toward success, as long as you persevere past the initial disappointment.

"Keep trying different things," Amy said, offering her best advice. "Keep going. I almost gave up, but I hadn't tried everything yet."

And while the fruits of the family's growing success have rewarded them in many ways, she closed our conversation by highlighting a particularly heartfelt moment. "It's always magical for parents when their kids say 'I love you,'" Amy told me. "But when you're working hard for them to use the minority language and, out of the blue, they say it to you in that language...it's like, wow. That's doubly magical."

AFTERWORD: Amy's family is a shining example of how discouraging results can actually propel parents forward to the goal of greater success. And the rewarding progress that Amy is experiencing with her children now also enables her to provide hard-won wisdom, through her blog and social media platforms, to other parents who may be feeling some discouragement of their own. But to get to this more fulfilling place, she and Juan had to overcome their early feelings of frustration by strategically reshaping their approach and redoubling their efforts to support their two minority languages more effectively. In other words, it's never too late for a course correction, and a more productive journey, but "interventions" of this kind will be most successful when they are pursued with the united front of *both* parents making this aim a higher priority for the family. While Amy and Juan are fortunate to share fluency in the same languages, couples who don't can still generate more satisfying progress by playing the most proactive roles they can to nurture their children's language development. What more can the minority language parent do? What more can the majority language parent do? How will they revise their efforts and how will they sustain their determination and drive from day to day? Such "interventions" may not be easy, and may demand considerable patience and perseverance, but greater success, on the other side, is indeed always possible.

CONTACT & RESOURCES FOR AMY

- ✉ ourmlhome@gmail.com
- 🌐 ourmlhome.wordpress.com (blog in English)
- 🌐 bilingue.home.blog (blog in French)
- f facebook.com/ourmlhome
- ℗ pinterest.fr/ourmlhome
- ⊙ @amy_ourmlhome
- 🐦 @Ourmlhome1

10

Strong Actions and Expectations Sustain the Minority Language

- ▶ Deborah is originally from Brazil and has lived in the U.S. for 12 years. She is fluent in her native Portuguese and in English. She is a stay-at-home mother and homeschools her two children.

- ▶ Her husband, Gentry, is American. He speaks English and has a limited passive understanding of Portuguese. He works as a firefighter.

- ▶ They have two sons: Frank, 7.2 years old, and Garrett, 4.5 years old.

- ▶ The family lives in San Diego.

Deborah had never been outside of Brazil when she came to the U.S. at the age of 27. She was planning to study English for a month at a language school in San Diego, then return to her work as a wellness coordinator in Sao Paulo...but ended up staying. "I fell in love with San Diego," she said. "When I got here, I just knew this was the place where I wanted to live. I didn't know the means to make that happen, but things just worked out right from the beginning."

Although Deborah had studied some English before coming to the U.S., she said that her speaking ability was still "really poor." This made her determined to improve and she became very proactive about her efforts to advance her English. "Even at school, there were many Brazilians and I wouldn't speak any Portuguese with anybody because I really wanted to learn English."

Twelve years later, now married and with two children, she said that her bilingual journey with her sons is similar to her own journey learning English. "It's very much the same approach, but in reverse," she said with a smile. "Now I only speak Portuguese! No English!"

Determined from the start

From the very beginning, Deborah's heart was set on communicating with her children in her native language. "That was most natural to me, speaking Portuguese to my children, even in the womb. To me, it just didn't feel right to speak anything but my native language to them from the time that they were conceived."

While Gentry has gradually gained some understanding of Portuguese since the time Frank was born, he's still unable to grasp much of the daily conversation taking place in this language. "It's just the way it's been," Deborah said. "I'm not very good at translating. Not that I don't have the ability to do it, but I guess I should care more about it. I feel like I put all of my effort into doing what I'm doing with my kids and I'm kind of letting the other pieces fall into place on their own."

Gentry, however, has been very supportive because he understands the importance of this aim to Deborah and to their children. Deborah called his support "a blessing," acknowledging that her quest would surely have been more difficult if he had been less understanding. "But I don't think it would have changed my determination because it's just what I decided to do and I'm kind of strong-willed."

Early on, though, she did encounter some concern from a family member, who was worried that Frank wouldn't develop sufficient ability in English if Deborah was only speaking to him in Portuguese. "Honestly, I wasn't concerned about this at all," she said. "I knew it was going to happen. I know how strong the English environment is and, to me, it's a battle every day just going against it."

Raising the odds of success

As Deborah predicted, Frank and Garrett have gained good proficiency in English at the same time as her efforts to nurture their Portuguese side are paying off. Now 7, Frank not only speaks both languages well, he's developing strong biliterate skills, too. "I don't know if I can say that it's on the same level as his growing ability in English, but I'm very satisfied with his growth in Portuguese," she said.

These rewarding results have been achieved despite a set of basic circumstances that, inherently, make the odds of success rather low. Such circumstances working against her bilingual aim include:

- Deborah is the primary source of exposure to Portuguese; her husband speaks only English.

- Deborah must communicate with her husband in English so the children are obviously aware that she's proficient in this language, too.

- They are immersed in an English-speaking society and don't often have the chance to travel back to Brazil.

The truth is, if Deborah hadn't been as proactive in her efforts to address these challenging conditions, she wouldn't have been able to raise the odds of success as high as she has. Her efforts, in fact, have managed to put the odds of success in her favor. They include:

1. Her unwavering commitment to speaking only Portuguese to her kids, both at home and out in the community.

2. Her firm expectations for her children to use Portuguese with her.

3. Her decision to pursue homeschooling.

4. Her efforts to expand their exposure to Portuguese, and Brazilian culture, beyond her own input.

Commitment to speaking only Portuguese

No matter the situation or setting, Deborah said she will only speak to her kids in the minority language, adding, "That's how it's been from the very beginning." And this is true not only in daily conversation, but in their homeschooling sessions as well. Although the boys are doing academic work in both English and Portuguese, Deborah herself always uses Portuguese when she addresses them.

Out in the city, too, Deborah remains persistent in her use of Portuguese with her children. "Even when we're in the park, or having a play date, if they're interacting in English with English-speaking kids, I'm still addressing my kids in Portuguese," she said.

When I asked if she has ever felt uncomfortable about using the minority language in public, she answered, "I haven't, no. If anything, I take pride in the Portuguese language. I love the language and I really want to expose them to it, as much as I can, whether we're at home or not. If it's not coming from me, then what's left? I'm the main source of that exposure and if I don't do it consistently, wherever we are, I feel like I'm not doing it right."

She then pointed out that her use of the minority language in public is not only beneficial to her bilingual aim, it can also create positive opportunities to connect with others. "I think people have been compassionate towards it. We take public transportation in San Diego all the time because I don't drive and people will ask, 'What language are you speaking?' So, if anything, I think it opens up different types of conversations with people and they start telling us about their experiences traveling the world or speaking a different language. It connects us."

As Deborah discussed her commitment to speaking only the minority language, she also mentioned a meeting that took place soon after she moved to the U.S. She said, "I met someone who was half-Brazilian. His mom was from Brazil and his dad was American. He was a grown man, 33 years old when I met him. He spoke Portuguese beautifully, but he wasn't taught Portuguese as a child. He told me, 'I had to work hard to learn the language. One of my biggest regrets was that my mom didn't speak Portuguese to me.' And that really stuck with me. I hadn't even met my husband then and I didn't have children, but that stuck with me."

Expectations for use of Portuguese

The fact that Deborah has been so consistent about using Portuguese with her children has not only helped fortify their language exposure, it has strengthened the conditions for them to continue communicating with her in this language despite the inherent lack of need to do so, given Deborah's ability in English. After all, if Deborah used English more freely with her kids, chances are they would feel more "permission" to use English with her.

As it is, she still faced this challenge of the child responding in the "wrong" language when Frank was small. "He wasn't even 4 years old when he started to reply to me in English," she said. "I made it really clear to him. I said in Portuguese, 'Frank, with mama, you only communicate in Portuguese. That's the only way.' I didn't really open up other choices. I didn't say, 'Okay, that's fine. Mama will continue to speak Portuguese to you whether you reply in Portuguese or not.' That's not how the conversation went. I made myself very clear that, with me, it would be Portuguese only."

She went on, "Maybe you could say it's an extreme approach, but I don't think they've been traumatized. They enjoy Portuguese, and they see the difference. They see kids whose parents are also from Brazil but can't speak Portuguese. So, from the beginning, when Frank started replying to me in English, I figured I needed to continue speaking to them in Portuguese consistently, but I also needed to step up my game in order to get them to continue using only Portuguese with me. This is when I came across your book, which was tremendously helpful in our bilingual journey going forward."

Thus, through this combination of extra effort to provide ample language exposure, while also standing firm on her expectations for her children's language use—in order to overcome the lack of need in these circumstances—Deborah was able to sustain their active use of the target language. "They've been conditioned to speak only Portuguese with me," she said.

Looking back on that challenging time with Frank, Deborah called it "a huge turning point" and added, "With my second child, Garrett, because he sees what Frank does, he was never really tempted to speak English with me because that's not the reality he's been experiencing from the beginning." Even when the activity itself is in English, she said, Garrett, like Frank, will turn to her and switch to Portuguese. "That's just the way we communicate," she said. "That's how we've learned to communicate together."

Decision to pursue homeschooling

Though Frank attended preschool for two years, when the time came to enroll him in kindergarten, Deborah said she had "mixed feelings" about it and her thoughts turned toward homeschooling. "There's no homeschooling in Brazil. It was just so different from what I had grown up with and from what I knew that I had never considered doing it. So it was never a part of our plan."

At that point, though, she realized, "If I sent my son off to school for seven hours a day, five days a week, learning Portuguese would be a lot more challenging. I felt like the odds would be more on my side if I homeschooled them. So the first thing was Portuguese, but I also wanted them to be able to spend time together, as brothers, and I wanted to open up their world a little more—like going places together and talking about things—than what it would have been like if they had gone to school."

She said she takes a "hybrid approach" to teaching her kids, pursuing subject matter in both English and Portuguese while continuing to communicate with them in Portuguese even when the content itself is in English. In terms of structure, the morning is their "school time" while the afternoon is given to "enrichment classes," including Capoeira, a type of Brazilian martial art; Brazilian jiu-jitsu; and "field trips," such as nature walks and regular visits to the local library and to city museums.

Efforts to expand language exposure

While Deborah's own efforts have gone a long way toward advancing her children's ability in Portuguese and their experience of Brazilian culture, she has extended these efforts even further through regular interactions with other Portuguese speakers.

Her twin sister moved to San Diego about four years ago and lives just five minutes away on foot. She frequently spends time with the boys, who enjoy "a special connection" with her. "It's made a big difference," Deborah said, "and not only regarding Portuguese. For them to be able to develop such a strong relationship with their aunt, it means the world to me."

Deborah added that she and her sister have done their best to introduce the boys to Brazilian cuisine by having them help make traditional Brazilian dishes at home. They also enjoy eating out at a Brazilian steakhouse in the city, where Portuguese is spoken and the restaurant is adorned with Brazilian flags. "It gives us the feeling of being closer to our home country," she said.

At the same time, Deborah keeps up a regular connection with her mother back in Brazil. Along with frequent online chats, they meet in person once or twice a year, with her mother visiting San Diego or the family meeting her halfway between their two locations, such as a spot in Mexico. Larger trips to Brazil have, so far, been limited. "Frank had just turned two the last time we visited Brazil, and Garrett was still in my womb," she said.

Beyond these interactions with other family members, Deborah has also sought out opportunities for additional language input by meeting up with a few local families whose children speak Portuguese and getting Frank and Garrett involved in activities, like the Capoeira and Brazilian jiu-jitsu "enrichment classes," where the teachers are Brazilian. Though most of the students are not Portuguese speakers, and so the classes are taught in English, Deborah asked the teachers to use Portuguese with her kids whenever possible. Thus, these once-a-week lessons not only contribute input in the minority language and culture, they reaffirm the value of Portuguese by showing the boys that others in their lives speak this language, too. "Every time we're there," Deborah said, "we get a little bit of Brazil to bring home."

Sustainable action for continuing progress

Asked about her advice for other parents, Deborah said, "I'd encourage them to continue speaking to their children in their native language, whatever it might be. Of course, it's their choice, but I see people all around me, parents who aren't from the U.S., and they're not doing that." Naturally, she can empathize with the difficulty of nurturing the minority language within a majority language environment, acknowledging that "The majority language is just so strong, and to go against that force, it does take a lot out of you." Still, she voiced agreement when I suggested that parents who don't make a sustainable effort to hand down their language, maybe some don't have later regrets, but others probably do. And the truth is, it's *always* possible for any parent to generate progress over time.

While they may not achieve the same success that they originally dreamed of, as long as they stick with it, they *will* be rewarded with continuing progress through the years of childhood.

Deborah also emphasized the importance of making ongoing efforts to bring suitable resources into the home as children grow, highlighting her home library of books in Portuguese and the additional Portuguese books she and the boys borrow from the local library on a weekly basis. She stressed the value of wordless picture books, too, by saying, "I can't overstate the power of storytelling. As we look at the illustrations together, they tell me the story in Portuguese, or we take turns telling the story."

Deborah added, though, that so far there is one type of resource that she has consciously decided to limit: digital devices. "We don't do screen time at home except for when we're doing schooling," she said. "I found, from the early years, that it was too addictive for Frank. I didn't want to deal with that. I thought it was counterproductive because even though he was learning from a video that was actually educational, he was getting addicted to the screen time. So I decided to eliminate that from our routine. During baseball season, they might watch some games with their dad at night, but other than that, we're not using it as a resource."

While Deborah's choices on her bilingual journey have generated satisfying progress for her and her children, she also recognizes that "each family has their own journey" to follow. When I asked how long her family would limit their use of digital devices, she replied, "As long as we can, and there's not a real struggle. Of course, we want to keep the dialogue open. We talk about things. We often have open conversations where our boys are given the chance to speak their minds."

"And when we can't decide for them," she concluded, "hopefully they'll make decisions based on what we've been giving them as a foundation for their lives."

AFTERWORD: The "odds of success" is an idea mentioned several times in Deborah's story. This means that, based on a family's particular circumstances, the inherent odds of success for fostering the child's active use of the minority language will be relatively higher or lower. For instance, if schooling is available in the minority language, this factor can strengthen the odds significantly. But when the family's circumstances suggest that the odds of success are not as promising, parents must do all that they can to fortify their conditions and efforts in order to nurture the minority language more effectively and raise those lower odds. Through her choices and actions, Deborah has done exactly that. At one point in her story, she used the word "extreme" when describing how some may view her actions. But the truth is, if the child's active use of the minority language is important to you, and the odds of success are inherently low, then "extreme" action—let's call it "passionate" action—may be what is needed to raise the odds high enough to actually fuel the success you seek. It's hard to say, of course, how "passionate" our actions must be to produce the desired outcome, but I think it's safe to say that erring on the side of stronger, more passionate action will invariably result in greater odds, and greater success, than erring in the other direction.

CONTACT FOR DEBORAH

✉ debignacio@hotmail.com

11

Commitment and Creativity Overcome the Odds and Tears

- ▶ Deepti is originally from India and has lived in the U.S. for 20 years. She is bilingual in Hindi and English and uses both languages in her work as an actor and audiobook narrator.
- ▶ Her husband, Larry, is American and monolingual in English. He is a writer.
- ▶ Their son, Josh, is 7.4 years old.
- ▶ Deepti speaks Hindi (and English) to Josh; Larry speaks English to Josh; Deepti and Larry communicate in English. Josh is also acquiring Spanish at school.
- ▶ The family lives in Los Angeles.

No language is universal, but perhaps the language of laughter comes closest.

When we hear pealing laughter from a conversation we can't understand, because we don't speak that language, we may not understand the context, but we understand the laughter. We understand the *joy*.

These were my thoughts while listening to an episode of the "Josh Ke Saath" storytelling podcast (joshkesaath.podbean.com). This is the podcast that Deepti has created with her young son, Josh, to engage him in Hindi, their minority language, while sharing their imaginative, made-up tales with other Hindi speakers in the world. Though I couldn't understand the words, I could understand the laughter, the joy.

Feeling determined from the start

Deepti grew up in Delhi and had a bilingual upbringing, with Hindi the main language at home and English the main language at school. In college she studied English Literature then left India to pursue a pair of Master's degrees, the first in Theater Studies in Singapore and the second in Acting in the U.S. It was in this program that she met Larry, who was studying playwriting.

"My plan was always to go back to India and teach or pursue acting there," Deepti said, "but then we met and we decided to get married. So we lived in New York for six years and now we've been in Los Angeles for nine years."

Before they had their son, Josh, Deepti was hopeful that Larry would learn Hindi, but the attempts they made did not bear much fruit. Finally, she came to the conclusion that "I just have to be okay with it. He's not going to be able to learn Hindi."

Although Deepti abandoned this aim with her husband, when she learned she was pregnant, the idea of handing down her mother tongue to her child became a goal that she was determined to realize. She explained, "I know people my age, their parents were immigrants from India and spoke the native language, but they don't. And they feel regret because they're part of that culture, but there's a language disconnect. So when they go to the home country, they connect but they don't—it's not an intimate connection to the culture. I wanted Josh to know me and know my family, not as a foreigner, but as one of us. And language was going to be an important part of it."

She also sensed, very early, that the overwhelming influence of the majority language and culture could threaten this deeply-felt goal if she didn't pursue it with as much passion as she could. The fact that Larry's side of the family was anticipating Josh's arrival with such excitement "woke up in me this understanding that if I don't create my side of his identity strongly, then it will get consumed by the majority culture that surrounds him."

Renegotiating language use at home

When Josh was born, her first words to him were in Hindi. "It was like, 'Oh, I have someone I can speak with in my language even though he doesn't know it or understand it, but he will.' It created a little unit within our nuclear family, which was, at times, challenging as well."

The challenge that Deepti refers to is one that many mixed couples face when one parent doesn't know the other's native language and may feel "excluded" from the communication taking place between the parent and child in that language. Intellectually, the "excluded" parent may support the bilingual aim, but emotionally, this daily dynamic can also cause some distress.

Recalling the first few weeks after Josh was born, Deepti said that Larry "felt like an outsider in his own family. He wanted me to translate everything for him. I was a new mom and having to translate all the things I was saying in Hindi got exhausting. So we had to renegotiate how our household would operate. There had to be times when he wouldn't know what I'm saying to our son and he would have to trust that when it was really important, I would switch to English to include him."

"Emotionally, that was challenging for both of us," she continued, "but I give my husband credit for supporting my efforts when my own family back in India didn't. My parents and relatives in India thought Josh had no need to learn Hindi since he lives in an English-speaking country. They didn't see a practical reason for investing all this energy into it. My husband's family, who don't speak Hindi, initially felt awkward when I'd speak to Josh in Hindi in front of them. I knew that they didn't understand what was being said and perhaps they felt left out. But to me, a child that's part of two cultures needs to have all the tools necessary to explore both cultures. And I felt it was my duty to give him the tool of Hindi."

Proactive efforts fuel progress

At the same time, Deepti has had to overcome several other significant challenges in order to advance her bilingual aim for her son. Not only is she largely the sole source of exposure to the minority language, she has continued to work from early on and this has affected the amount of input in Hindi that Josh receives.

"Up until the age of 2," she said, "he was at home with us because we were both freelancing. But at the time I was still traveling a lot for work and so, for those four or five days, he would be alone with Larry and it was only English. All that time I was spending away from him, he was also spending that time away from the language."

Her frustration grew further when Josh began attending pre-school and came home speaking more and more English. "I was like, 'Oh my God, what do I do now?' The feeling of being alone on this journey became overwhelming, and I worried constantly about his losing Hindi."

At that point, Deepti realized she would need to be even more proactive, even more resourceful. Taking her cue from the English that surrounded him at school, she made efforts to enrich their home with more Hindi, seeking out more Hindi resources—books, games, music, videos, apps—and even creating some of her own, like Hindi blocks, which she and Josh fashioned from a set of alphabet blocks by pasting Hindi letters onto them.

Along with the stronger efforts she was making at home to provide input and add to their resources, Deepti continued their annual custom, since Josh was a baby, of taking him to India for about three weeks each summer. There, among family and friends, he can be immersed in the language and culture and feel a "practical need," she said, for Hindi.

"I remember when he was 3 years old and we were in Delhi. He was playing with some kids on the playground and they were on this little merry-go-round. One kid told another kid a joke and Josh laughed and I was like, he totally knew, not just the words, he also got the humor. He may not be reproducing it right now, but he knows it and little proofs like this were really important markers for me to continue on. These are the sort of moments that have given me courage and hope."

At that point, then, Deepti's communication with Josh may have been mostly one-sided in the sense that she would generally speak in Hindi to him and he would generally respond in English to her. But she also recognized that her efforts were indeed fueling his growing language acquisition, that she was "on the right path," as she put it. She likened this to the process of his development of Spanish at the Spanish immersion school he has attended since kindergarten. As the principal of the school pointed out to her, children who have no previous exposure to Spanish will first go through a stage of understanding the language before they're able to actually speak it. "Hearing that," she said, "I was like, 'Oh, that's kind of what his journey in Hindi has been like.'"

Creating more opportunity for output

Over the next several years, Deepti sought out more situations for Josh to make use of his Hindi side. She made connections with other Indian families in the area who view Hindi as a priority for their children and she enrolled him in a weekly Hindi class with other kids. Along with the language exposure and engagement that these experiences have offered, Deepti feels that Josh has also benefited from realizing that "there are other kids like me, other kids learning Hindi, too."

One of those kids, in fact, is Josh's cousin. Deepti's sister is married to a French man and they live in France with their young daughter, around the same age as Josh. Because the strongest language the two children share is Hindi, Hindi thus becomes the language they use together when the families meet.

Deepti's persistent efforts were generating progress, but, compared to English and Spanish, she still felt there was a lack of opportunity for Josh to actively use Hindi. "His Spanish was getting stronger and there was more reading and writing in Spanish at school. There was output in that language and I was like, 'Oh, where's the Hindi output?' I'm talking to him a lot in Hindi and he answers me in Hindi, but it's not completely consistent. And I'm reading books to him, or he's watching something, but there's no output. So the podcast came as a way to encourage him to articulate his ideas in Hindi so that that part of his brain gets activated in that language."

A playful and productive activity

At the time I spoke to Deepti, she and Josh had already been producing their weekly podcast episodes for nearly a year. For each episode, which they usually record on Saturday morning, they sit in front of a microphone and spontaneously make up a story that lasts around 15 or 20 minutes. These stories are based on a "story starter"—often submitted by listeners from their audience—which consists of a "who" (a goat, for example), a "what" (playing ping-pong), and a "where" (at the Olympics). Mother and son, speaking back and forth in Hindi, improvise these stories together, building on each other's contributions. "Even if we falter in speaking Hindi to each other during the week, I know that this is a dedicated time that we will," she said.

While the spirited stories they produce often prompt laughter during the podcast recording, Deepti admits that, behind the scenes, it can sometimes be a challenge to sustain Josh's motivation for the activity, even though he enjoys it. Like any child, Josh can be drawn to a new book or toy, which ends up throwing off their Saturday morning podcast time and Deepti's own schedule. Yet, remembering the commitment she and Josh made to pursue this project for at least a year, she sets aside her frustration and continues "trying to figure out how to keep him engaged."

Deepti said that their storytelling podcast has had a positive impact in a range of ways: advancing Josh's language ability while stretching his imagination and creativity; deepening their own bond as parent and child; and offering inspiration to other Hindi speakers who listen in to their podcast episodes. She described receiving grateful responses from families in many parts of the world, then added, "I share these messages with Josh because I want him to know that he's having an impact on other kids' lives, kids like him. He enjoys it when he finds out that, 'Oh, this kid in India is listening to this fun story we just made or this other kid in England listens to the podcast on his way to his Hindi class. Sometimes I need that to keep me on task even on days when it's challenging and he keeps wanting to postpone it. And I'm like, 'We made a promise to each other, right? So let's do it!'"

Pressing on, past the tears

I asked Deepti how well Josh can now communicate in Hindi and she replied, "I would say 80% of the time, he can. Every now and then, there might be certain ideas that are more formed in English in his brain. So to bring them into Hindi—even I have challenges with that sometimes because I've learned to parent here in English.

So sometimes it's like, 'Oh wait, how do I navigate that in Hindi?' But 80% of the time, he's good."

To reach this rewarding point in her journey with Josh, Deepti has had to overcome a variety of difficulties often faced by parents in situations where the odds of success are inherently low. Among them: the minority language is a less common language in her location; her son's exposure to the minority language depends almost entirely on her own efforts and yet she's also working; the majority language must be used to communicate with her partner; and the task of finding useful resources in the minority language has been an ongoing struggle (and has forced her to compromise on allowing more screen time than she otherwise would have liked in order to provide more Hindi input). "There are many times I've cried," she said, "just feeling like, 'Why am I doing this? This is so hard.'"

Yet Deepti has pressed on, beyond these tears, and is finding considerable success and joy on the other side of her challenges. Explaining her perseverance, she said, "For me, I can't even say it's important—it's essential. Maybe it starts intellectually, but it has to grow into a necessity, which is the only way to really sustain the long term."

She then shared a story that keenly underscores this point, telling me, "I was working on a project this summer and there were two young men in their twenties. They were born in the UK, but their parents are from India and they knew their parents' language up until the age of 7—the age Josh is now. But once they were in elementary school, the parents didn't keep it up and now the kids don't know it. That really reinforced for me, like, 'Until he goes to college, I'm going to be on it!' Because otherwise, it's so easy to give up."

AFTERWORD: Deepti, too, has had to contend with very challenging circumstances to advance her bilingual aim. In her case, the proactive efforts she has made have also involved creative projects that serve to engage her son in the minority language, of which the podcast is the most prominent example. To my mind, one of the most powerful and fulfilling ways of promoting the target language is through a creative vehicle which weds the parent's own personal passions with an activity that can generate enthusiastic engagement in that language. An actor and audiobook narrator, Deepti has followed the call of her own creative spirit, and her desire to nurture Josh's Hindi side, by starting and sustaining this playful podcast. The podcast also shows how creative actions of this kind not only can benefit parent and child, if shared with the world in some way, they may offer compelling value to others as well. Creative projects, whether short-term efforts or longer-running activities, can enable parents to pursue the enlivening idea of empowering the minority language through actions that unleash their own creative spirit, and, in turn, even enrich the lives of many more. Creating a podcast or a video or a book—these are just a few of the ways that parents and children can engage in fun, productive activities that fuel greater success and joy on the bilingual journey.

CONTACT & RESOURCES FOR DEEPTI

- ✉ joshkesaath@gmail.com
- 🌐 joshkesaath.podbean.com
- 🌐 deeptigupta.com
- 🌐 deeptiguptanarrates.com
- 🅕 facebook.com/TheDeeptiGupta
- 🅞 @TheDeeptiGupta
- 🐦 @TheDeeptiGupta

12

Passion for the Minority Language, Compassion for Our Children

- ▸ Ana is originally from Colombia and has lived in the U.S. for 10 years. Her mother tongue is Spanish and she is also proficient in English. She is the founder of Spanish Plus Me (spanishplusme.com), a musical approach to language learning, and the creator of the album *Short + Fun Spanish Beats*.

- ▸ Her husband, Bryan, is American and is a monolingual English speaker. He works for a tech company.

- ▸ Ana and Bryan have two children: a son, Samuel, 8.8 years old, and a daughter, Sarah, 5.8 years old.

- ▸ The family lives in northern California.

Bilingualism has been a guiding light in Ana's life from the time she was a child in Colombia.

"My parents believed in bilingualism so they always tried to expose us to the English language," she said. "My dad said that being bilingual was going to give us opportunities. That was his goal so my parents always enrolled us in schools where they taught English."

By the time Ana graduated from college, where she studied Mass Media and Journalism, she had developed a strong level of English ability. "I was kind of bilingual, supposedly, but you sometimes discover that you're not that bilingual when you go out of the country. I was working in public relations, for a public relations agency, and because I was able to communicate in English and write in English my bosses would assign me clients and accounts from American companies."

In this way, Ana was given the account of an American software design company and had to travel to the U.S. for a meeting with the marketing and sales team. And it was there, at that meeting, that she met Bryan, who was working in the company's sales department in California. Ana recalled, "When we first met, he started the conversation with '¡Hola! ¿Cómo está?' I thought he could speak Spanish so I said, 'Muy bien. ¿Y tú?' And he said, 'No, no! I don't speak Spanish! That's all the Spanish I know!' Later we went out for a drink with some other people and at the end we exchanged email addresses. After that, we started communicating through Messenger and Skype."

For the next several years, Ana and Bryan then maintained a long-distance relationship by visiting each other as often as they could manage and speaking frequently via video chats. And as their bond deepened, they began discussing marriage and children. "I remember we were talking and he was like, 'There's something I want you to know: I want our kids to be bilingual. I can't speak any other language myself and I really want them to be bilingual.' And I was like, 'Yeah, of course. But we have no idea how to do it!'"

Finally, they married and Ana moved to the United States so that the couple could begin their new life together there.

Support from her husband and his family

While Bryan's Spanish is still limited, like many majority language parents who began with little or no knowledge of the minority language, he has gradually gained some ability over time. Even without actively studying the language, such parents are able to pick up a certain amount of passive understanding, and even active use, from being "immersed" in this language at home and spending time in the minority language country.

"He definitely has improved," Ana said. "Now, after 10 years, he'll sometimes ask for something in Spanish or he'll address the kids with a bit of Spanish. He's feeling more confident. When we go to Colombia, he can order a meal or ask for directions. He says he can understand some conversations—but, of course, when everyone is talking at their native speed, it's very difficult."

Still, Ana said that Bryan has been very easygoing about *not* being able to understand. At one point she asked him if he ever feels left out and he told her that it wasn't a concern for him. "That's probably his personality. I think there are other men that are a little more like, 'Oh, I want to know what you're saying to my child.' The thing is, he has his own close relationship with our kids in English so he doesn't feel that his relationship with them is affected in any way. I know there are some parents that feel left out, but in my husband's case, he's super relaxed."

Ana credits Bryan's positive attitude—along with the moral support of his extended family—for enabling her efforts to proceed as productively as they have over the years. "He believes in this," she said. "When the spouse doesn't really believe in the journey, it's much more difficult. But he loves the idea, to the point that his family believes in it, too. I've heard very sad stories where the in-laws don't agree or aren't supportive, so I feel very blessed. Last year I asked my in-laws, 'Have you ever felt left out because of me speaking Spanish with the kids around you?' And their response was very beautiful. They said, 'Ana Maria, we are so proud that our grandchildren can be bilingual.'"

Speaking Spanish out in public

Given their circumstances, Ana and Bryan settled into the OPOL approach from early on. When Ana became pregnant with Samuel, the couple began addressing her belly in their native languages. "Bryan was talking and reading to the baby in English," she said, "and I would take my guitar and sing in Spanish."

This consistency then continued after Samuel was born. Ana developed the habit of switching back and forth between Spanish with Samuel and English with Bryan, her in-laws, and other English speakers. And though some parents struggle with the experience of speaking to their children in the minority language when out in public, Ana persisted, buoyed by the fact that her own bilingualism has been such an asset to her life and that she was "very proud of being bilingual."

"So speaking Spanish with my kids has never been embarrassing for me or made me feel less," she said. "What I've learned, though, after living here for 10 years, is that there are other circumstances that could make a mother in the U.S. think twice before speaking in Spanish with her child in public. But I've never experienced a difficult situation with this. I've never seen rolling eyes or anything. I've been very lucky."

Cultivating her own community

For the first few years, Ana was unable to find convenient Spanish activities for small children in her area so she took Samuel to English activities that included a story time and classes in music, art, and swimming. During these activities, she would continue interacting with Samuel in Spanish.

When Samuel was 3 and a half, the family moved to a new city and Ana resumed her search for Spanish activities, but again found that there were no options nearby.

"That was when it clicked," Ana recalled. "I said, you know what? I'm going to do something in Spanish with the friends we have. I'm going to teach Spanish to my kids' friends. In this way, at least our friends will learn some Spanish and we can meet more people who care about bilingualism. It's okay if they don't speak Spanish. If they want to learn, that will affect us, too."

So Ana opened her own class, with stories and songs and other activities in Spanish. Starting with her own family—her children were now 4 and 1—and other families in the neighborhood, she was able to cultivate a growing community for her minority language. What's more, she could charge a fee for her weekly class and provide some support to her family in this way, too.

Creating her own music

When Ana first opened the class, she wanted to use Spanish songs that she felt were suitable for the needs of the group, but struggled to find what she wanted. This obstacle then led to the idea of creating her own songs, which could be tailored for her class. Stressing that she plays guitar at a "basic level," she nevertheless picked it up and began composing "the introductory song, the bye-bye song, and the movement song. Then it was Halloween, so I created something with pumpkins. And then it was Earth Day, so I created a song for Earth Day. So that's how it started. And the kids and parents loved them."

As the number of original songs grew, and she continued to receive positive feedback from her class, Bryan eventually encouraged her to record an album of her music. Ana happened to have a friend from Colombia, also now living in the U.S., who works professionally as a music producer. But even at a reduced rate for his work, it was still a costly project and, at first, Ana declined.

Three years passed. During this time she closed her Spanish class and began volunteering as a Spanish teacher at her children's school, where she continued to successfully use her songs. Finally, despite her reservations about the cost, she decided to move forward with the idea of creating her own album to introduce Spanish to children.

This meant, however, that she would have to fly from California to Florida, where her friend lived, and spend a week there to record the songs. And because of a misunderstanding, Bryan had scheduled a business trip during that same week she had planned to travel. "So my parents came from Colombia to stay with the kids, but two days before they arrived, my son broke his arm. It was a nightmare. I'm leaving my kids for the first time, my son has a broken arm, and Bryan's not going to be here, either. But I said, 'I have to do this!' I cried on the airplane, but I went."

And it turned out that Ana not only was able to realize her dream of making the album, she found that the whole experience was deeply empowering. "For me, this project goes much further than whatever it means in music and business," she said. "It changed my life."

The positive impact of her work

With the album recorded, Ana then created a website, Spanish Plus Me, to share her songs and her musical approach to engaging children in Spanish. The album, titled *Short + Fun Spanish Beats*, is available online at all digital music stores and streaming services.

Asked about the impact of her work since then, Ana told me that she has enjoyed additional opportunities to visit local schools and share her music and the benefits of bilingualism. "I want to help kids get a different perception of languages," she said. "Not only the Spanish language. When I go into a classroom, I talk to kids about being bilingual, about what it means to learn another language. If they understand what bilingualism is and why it's important, then their perception of other languages, like Spanish, will change, too."

She continued, "So before we start singing, I tell them my story as a bilingual, not about Spanish per se, but how being bilingual can change your life and how far it can take you. Basically, I try to teach the kids more about bilingualism and I encourage them to learn another language. And after that I say, 'Okay, now who wants to learn a little more Spanish?' And they're like, 'Me!' And then we start singing."

Naturally, Ana's passion for her music and for bilingualism have also had a very positive impact on her own children. They take pride in the fact that their mother has been involved in their schools and that they have been able to follow in her bilingual footsteps. Recounting some English homework that Samuel once did, Ana said, "He had to write an answer to the question 'What do you like about yourself?' and he said: 'I like my clothes, I like my shoes, and I like that I can speak another language.'"

Siblings around the world often come to rely mainly on the majority language to communicate between themselves, and in this respect, Samuel and Sarah are no different: they mainly use English. However, they continue to switch to Spanish when communicating with Ana, even though they're well aware that she's also proficient in English. "I believe there's an emotional connection with Spanish," she explained. "If you don't create that emotional connection with the language, with you as the source of that language, I think it's difficult. So make your target language the language of love with your kids, the language in which you connect with your children."

Ana pointed to the fact that she has always been very consistent about "switching gears" and speaking Spanish to her kids, and has done her best, day after day, to make their experience of Spanish enjoyable by engaging with her kids in playful ways. "Make it fun," she said. "I always say this. Make it fun, and be flexible. I know it's important to be consistent, but also be—and these are words I've been using lately—compassionate and empathetic. They're kids. We also have to listen to their needs and it's about finding whatever works for your family. If you ask what has worked for me—to create that emotional connection—it's being a mom in Spanish, not being a teacher of Spanish. I'm trying to be a mom in Spanish."

Having both passion and compassion

While Ana is pleased with her children's progress, she also takes a realistic view of their bilingual development. "Of course, I see that their English is getting stronger than their Spanish, but I decided not to worry about that. I'll be honest with you. In the beginning, I probably set the bar higher, but I decided to lower it a little bit. I wanted to be more relaxed. Their Spanish isn't perfect, but at this moment, it's not my priority for them to be perfect bilinguals. For me, it's more important that they love it, that they don't feel embarrassed, that they feel proud of being bilingual. It's more important that they actually want, at least, to speak in Spanish. If their Spanish isn't perfect, they can always continue learning it. We can find other ways to do it when they're older."

Summing up her perspective on the bilingual journey, Ana again emphasized the importance of compassion: while we need to be passionate about our bilingual aim, we must also be compassionate toward our children. "That little kid wants to connect with you," she said. "You may want your child to be bilingual, but your child also needs to feel like mommy's there, and daddy's there, no matter the language."

AFTERWORD: Ana's story keenly demonstrates how fruitful a little determination can be when it comes to seeking ways to expand our children's exposure to the minority language. Responding to the lack of Spanish opportunities in her local community, she rose above her frustrations by creating her own opportunity: a Spanish class for young kids. And this class not only benefited her own family, it benefited other families as well. In fact, because of this class, she also began writing songs which eventually led to her recording project—another good example of personal passion expressing itself in a creative form for greater language learning. Her music then brought her into classrooms to offer an encouraging taste of bilingualism to many more children. Ana's original spark of determination, in other words, gradually caught fire in a variety of enjoyable and effective ways. And it's important to note, as Ana told me, that she doesn't consider herself to be a "professional musician." But she took her interest in music and has made the most of it—overcoming plenty of obstacles along the way—to advance her bilingual aim for her kids and her desire to promote bilingualism more broadly. At the same time, she maintains a healthy mindset in balancing her passion for bilingual success with compassion for the reality of her children's lives.

CONTACT & RESOURCES FOR ANA

- ✉ spanishplusme@gmail.com
- 🌐 spanishplusme.com
- 🇫 facebook.com/spanishplusme
- 🇫 facebook.com/anacalabresebeats
- 📷 @anacalabrese_spm (English)
- 📷 @anacalabrese_enespanol (Spanish)
- 📷 @reddeapoyo_crianzabilingue (founding member of this support network for expat families with Spanish as a minority language)
- ♪ *Short + Fun Spanish Beats* (album of children's music)

13

Love of Books and Reading Fuels Language Ability and Literacy

- ▶ Mayken is originally from Germany and has lived in France for over 20 years. Along with her native German, she is fluent in French and English. She works for a property management company.

- ▶ Her husband, Gérald, is French. He speaks French and has developed passive ability in German. He works as a buyer for a French car company.

- ▶ Their daughter, Lanna, is 9.2 years old.

- ▶ Mayken speaks German (and some English) to Lanna; Gérald speaks French to Lanna; and Mayken and Gérald communicate in French.

- ▶ The family lives in Paris.

Mayken has long had an interest in languages beyond her native German. Along with fluency in French and English, she has growing ability in Italian and studied Russian when she was younger. Recalling her days as a university student, when she wrote her diploma thesis on a topic involving kindergarten children and second language learning, she said, "That's when I knew for sure that if I ever had children, I wanted to raise them bilingual."

While living in Paris, Mayken met Gérald (through their mutual love of rollerskating) and eventually they married and felt ready to have children. "Even though he was French and spoke only French, he was on board right away," she recalled. "He said, 'Yes, of course. Our children will be bilingual.'"

In fact, Mayken and Gérald now have a trilingual aim for their 9-year-old daughter, Lanna. While French and German are the family's main two languages, and have naturally been given the greater amount of attention, Mayken has also been making efforts to nurture Lanna's acquisition of English.

"I want her to be comfortable in both French and German," Mayken said. "In reading and writing, too. And I want her to be comfortable in English as well. I'd like her to get started early, have fun with English, and meet a lot of people she wouldn't otherwise be able to meet. I have a lot of friends with whom I communicate in English. I want Lanna to be able to do the same."

Early efforts pay off in active ability

From the time Lanna was born, Mayken and Gérald have used the OPOL approach: Mayken speaks German to her and Gérald speaks French. French is also the couple's shared language "because his knowledge of German was very basic to start with. Now he has a pretty good understanding, except when it's a very complicated issue. But it's mostly understanding and not so much speaking."

As Mayken keenly appreciated the fact that she was largely the sole source of exposure to German, she felt driven to be especially proactive when Lanna was small. "I went back to work when she was 4 months old," Mayken explained, "and she was full-time with a French childminder. At age 3, she started preschool, our neighborhood preschool."

Yet, despite these circumstances—French at home from Gérald and from the interactions between Gérald and Mayken, and French from daycare and preschool—Mayken's persistent efforts to provide Lanna with exposure to German fostered an early foundation of active ability in this language. "I felt pretty good," she said, "because she was doing really well and she was talking to me in German even though she heard me speaking in French."

She acknowledged that this had been a worry, that Lanna might have begun relying more on the majority language to communicate, as can be the case with children in such circumstances. "But it just never happened. She always stuck to German." Mayken suggests that this result was due not only to the conditioning created by her own efforts, but to her daughter's personality as well, in her willingness to accept and abide by certain "rules" around her, at home and at school. "Maybe she says to herself, 'Okay, that's the way it is and that's the way we do it.' She didn't question it and now it's become natural."

Still, like many parents hustling to provide their children with exposure to the minority language, Mayken was both pleased with the progress her daughter was making and yet continuously wondering, as she put it, "What more can I do?" In addition, she admitted to feeling some jealousy over the circumstances of other families she knew, where the German-speaking parents had more time to spend with their children or the children had a German caregiver or attended a German bilingual school of some kind.

And so, while Lanna was still in preschool, Mayken and Gérald began exploring the idea of placing her in a bilingual school to supplement Mayken's efforts and enable her to breathe a bit more easily.

Gaining a spot in a bilingual school

"There are few options for German in the Paris area," Mayken said, "and practically speaking, it's a matter of how much it costs and where the school is located."

As it turned out, the only realistic option for their family was a school in the heart of Paris which offers, within its French curriculum, five weekly hours of classes in German for German speakers. (The school also offers classes in English for English speakers, making it a dual bilingual program.)

To their great delight, they were able to gain one of the few spots available in the German section for Lanna. When the school called with the good news and told Mayken that they wanted to make an appointment to complete the registration, perhaps the following week, she recalled replying: "How about tomorrow!"

Lanna, then, entered this school at the age of 5 and will continue going there—and receiving additional exposure to German on a regular basis—up through high school.

When I asked Mayken to imagine how her journey would have been different if Lanna had not been able to enter this bilingual program, she said, "I think we would have spent every available school holiday in Germany and now we're a bit more relaxed about it. We still go to Germany frequently, but we take summer holidays somewhere else."

Books and reading form a cornerstone

Having Lanna attend a bilingual school is certainly helpful to Mayken's bilingual aim, but she realizes that five hours a week of German doesn't free her from the need to continue making her own proactive efforts. She added, "We had to sign an agreement with the school that says that if her German is not up to a certain level, she won't be able to continue in that program. So the teachers emphasize that it's only five hours a week and we still have to do a lot of work at home."

Toward that end, books and reading have long been a cornerstone of her efforts to promote the minority language. "I've been a bookworm all my life," she said. "I learned to read before I started school because my mom read me stories and, at some point, I just started watching where her finger was in the book and I learned to read that way."

Mayken has followed her mother's example by reading aloud to Lanna since the time she was a baby. She even reads to her twice a day, in the morning and in the evening. On school days, she used to read to her at home, after breakfast, for 10 or 15 minutes before they left the house for school. But after a recent move, to a location farther away, the commute to school has grown longer and they have to leave the house earlier. Mayken now makes use of this time they spend riding the Metro by maintaining their read-aloud routine—in a quieter voice, perhaps—right there on the subway train. She is equally persistent about their routine at bedtime, noting, "We drop it only if there's a special event and we get home really late at night."

For herself, Mayken mainly reads e-books on a digital device, "but for my daughter, I still buy real books. We tried to read an e-book together, but she gets really distracted by all the options on the reader, like making the type bigger and turning the pages. So I think that physical books are still a lot better."

From the hundreds and hundreds of books in the family's Paris apartment, Mayken would seem to agree with my own maxim that "You can never have too many books!" Majority language partners, however, aren't always as enthusiastic about the minority language parent's eager book-buying ways. She admits that her husband's response to seeing yet another new stack of books—from online orders, bookshops, or trips back to Germany—is sometimes, "Oh no, not more books!" But Mayken cheerfully counters, "We can fit them in somewhere!"

Additional input through captive reading

Along with all the language input that she provides from this ever-expanding collection of books, Mayken makes the most of a strategy that I call "captive reading." With this tactic, the parent regularly posts some suitable text—like a short story or article—in a "captive location" where the child will see it and naturally attempt to read it. As I've done with my own kids for years, Mayken posts this material in the bathroom, by the toilet, and changes it every few days. When this strategy is pursued with persistence, year after year from the time the child is first learning to read, the additional exposure—without the parent even needing to be present—can play a significant part in advancing the child's language ability, literacy development, and background knowledge of the world.

Mayken mentioned three different types of text that have been effective in her "captive reading" efforts with Lanna. About the first, short fiction, she explained, "I try to find a short story on the internet and print it out in big type. Recently, I've tried detective stories, where there's a question at the end—who did it and what is the clue? And I wait for her to give me the clue before I confirm the answer. That way, I know she reads the whole story."

The second type of text is nonfiction related to Lanna's interests. "I found a website with information on animals and I choose the animals that she's interested in, like cats and wolves and bats. These articles are on several pages so I'll ask her, 'Have you finished reading that page?' and then I'll give her the next page."

And the third type of text is nonfiction connected to personal needs in her daughter's life. Mayken told me that Lanna had to take a test in Germany about various practical rules when going swimming, like how to react in the event of a thunderstorm. "So when we were planning to go to Germany," she said, "I looked up the rules on the internet and found a very nice presentation with pictures. Then I put that up in the bathroom for her to look at and we talked about it." Mayken went on to say that Lanna passed the test with flying colors and she was proud of her for being able to explain these rules, in her own words, to the lifeguard who tested her.

The benefits of travel and pen pals

Annual trips to Germany—during the summer and at Christmas, for a week or two at a time—have also been an important part of Mayken's efforts to promote both the German language and culture, while enabling Lanna to bond with her grandparents and other family members. Mayken has even managed to arrange for her daughter to spend a day or two, year after year, at an elementary school in her hometown—in fact, it was *her* elementary school when she was a child. "I thought, well, I don't have anything to lose. I'll just contact the school and say I'm a former student. If they say yes, they say yes and that's great. And if they say no, well then, at least I've tried."

As it turns out, this proactive step has resulted not only in a variety of memorable experiences for Lanna at a German school, it also led to an ongoing friendship between her and a German girl of the same age who lives right next door to Mayken's mother. "Whenever we're at my mom's, she wants to go over and play. And if we're just there for two or three days, she'll say, 'Can I at least go over and say hello?'"

Summing up this fruitful experience, she said, "So all kinds of things developed out of this—from my first initiative of thinking that maybe she could attend a day at my old elementary school—and then it all spiraled out from there."

At the same time, Mayken was eager to connect Lanna with pen pals in Germany, too. "Pen pals were a big thing for me when I was a kid," she said, describing how she enjoyed writing letters in English and French and is still even in touch with some of her childhood pen pals today. "I thought it would be a nice thing to do for my daughter so when she was old enough and writing comfortably, not struggling with each letter, I started thinking about pen pals for her."

Through The Bilingual Zoo, Mayken was able to find Lanna's first pen pal—the son of another member of this forum—and that parent then suggested a second pen pal, a girl who went to school with her son.

"My daughter loves getting their letters," Mayken said. "It's a bit harder to get her to write, to motivate her to write back, but I tell her, 'Look how much you love getting a letter. Imagine your friend getting a letter and being just as excited about it as you are. So don't you want to sit down and start writing? You have so much to tell since the last letter.'" She went on to explain how she then helps Lanna improve her draft and finally has her write the letter on proper paper.

Encouraging progress in English, too

Although Mayken's main focus has naturally been on nurturing her daughter's ability in German, she has also been taking some steps to encourage progress in Lanna's third language, English, through a combination of extracurricular opportunities at school and her own efforts at home. Some English-speaking friends, too, have been engaging sources of input, both in France and overseas. Mayken recounted a recent trip that she and Lanna took to Canada, where they spent time with friends who have children that are similar in age and have similar interests, like Harry Potter—but these children only speak English.

"They have a girl who's a year older than Lanna," Mayken said, "and when we arrived on the evening of the first day, the girls just hit it off right away, but without talking—they were making animal noises, like they were howling like wolves. So the whole evening, it was very funny. And then, after that, they actually started communicating. We went camping for two days, and to a safari park, and the other girl was in my car with us—the two girls were in the back seat. They would play together and we had about three days where they were together all the time. And, of course, we were talking only in English—only her and me in German and all the rest was in English."

For Mayken, whether the target language is German or English, her attitude toward progress is the same. "You have to be consistent and persistent," she said. "Like you're in it for the long run. And you really have to do it every day. Not like, 'Oh no, today I'm tired, I don't feel like it.' You have to do it every day, day by day, and it'll add up."

AFTERWORD: Like many families enjoying success on their bilingual or multilingual journey, books and reading—lots of books and lots of reading—have played a powerful role in the progress experienced by Mayken's family. In fact, I can personally attest to this because I had the pleasure of spending a few days with her family in France. While their apartment in Paris bears little resemblance to our house in Hiroshima, in two basic ways they're very much the same: though the living space is limited, books are in abundance. And our kinship for books in two far-flung locations reminded me of the international study *Family scholarly culture and educational success: Books and schooling in 27 nations*, published in 2010 in the journal *Research in Social Stratification and Mobility*. This massive study, which analyzed the lives of some 70,000 people, revealed—even given the parents' level of education and occupation, as well as such factors as gender, class, nationality, political system, and gross national product—that the impact of books is the same throughout the world: *Children in families with a large home library (defined in the study as 500 or more books) experience significantly greater educational success...and, naturally, success in schooling is a direct outgrowth of success in language development.* The study even goes on to say that "the taste for books" is handed down from generation to generation, which means that if you build a large home library for your children, not only will it benefit their upbringing, they'll likely build a large home library themselves one day that will benefit their own kids!

CONTACT FOR MAYKEN

✉ m.bruenings@web.de

14

Minority Language Family Still Faces Challenging Conditions

- Izabela and her husband, Tomasz, are originally from Poland. They moved to a small city in England in 2005. Izabela speaks Polish and English and helps run her family's business selling Polish books, called *Czytam i mówię po polsku* (czytamimowiepopolsku.com/gb/).

- Tomasz speaks Polish and English and works at an automotive company.

- They have two sons who were born in England: Adam, 10.6 years old, and Oliver, 4.6 years old. The boys attend regular English-speaking schools.

When both parents are speakers of the minority language, and they speak this language at home to their children, and with each other, such circumstances are among the most conducive conditions for realizing success on the bilingual journey. Still, this sort of advantageous situation—the approach known as "minority language at home" (ml@home)—doesn't guarantee that everything will be smooth sailing. As Izabela has discovered, advancing her children's ability in Polish, and sustaining their active use of this language, has demanded additional efforts beyond the family's daily interactions.

After Poland joined the European Union in 2004, a large wave of Polish people came to the UK to establish new lives here over the years that followed. Among them were Izabela's parents and brother as well as Izabela and her husband, Tomasz. Their children—Adam, 10, and Oliver, 4—were born in the UK.

Izabela told me, "I want my children to be able to speak in Polish freely, to communicate with me, my family, and with my husband's family back in Poland. So speaking is very important, and I also want them to be able to read and write in Polish, but I see how that's more difficult than speaking. So we put a lot of effort into making sure that they're fluent in Polish, but I can see how, for them, it's more natural to use English than Polish. For them, Polish is a second language."

Focusing on Polish within the family

The effort Izabela refers to includes maintaining Polish as the family's shared language—with some exceptions for the use of English—and keeping up a regular bedtime reading routine. "Most of the time, Tomasz and I speak Polish to them. We only speak English if we have guests or when we go to school and talk to their teachers or other parents, things like that. I also read to the boys every day and I make sure it's always a Polish book."

In addition to this daily input and interaction in the target language, the fact that Izabela's parents live in a nearby city means that Adam and Oliver have frequent opportunities to spend time with their grandparents and speak Polish. Izabela said that the boys tend to stick to Polish when communicating with them because, although the grandparents can speak English, they generally use only Polish around the children. "When the children are with me," Izabela explained, "they'll be a bit lazy with it sometimes. They'll use English phrases because they know I'll understand. They see me talking to other people in English a lot. But their granny, they don't see her speaking to other people in English. My mum was saying the other day that when they went to the cinema with Adam, she was ordering popcorn and Adam was so surprised to see her speaking in English!"

Further support from the Polish community

The helpful influence of other family members also extends to the larger Polish community. "There are about one million Polish people living in the UK," she said. "There are a lot of Polish people here everywhere you go. There are Polish shops in small towns like ours as well as a Polish Saturday school." The Saturday school, Izabela said, is a structured way for Polish residents in the UK and in countries around the world to hand down their language and culture to their children. At the same time, for Polish kids attending these schools, "the fact that they see other children speaking in Polish, that's very positive for them because they see, 'Oh, I'm not alone in this. There are so many other people like me.'"

Although Adam eventually put up some resistance to going to the Polish Saturday school, not wanting another day of school on Saturday, Izabela was able to maintain his attendance by giving him a choice between the Saturday school and an online school. When Adam tried the online school for a year, and found that it wasn't a good fit, he then opted to return to the Saturday school. "So it was his decision to go back and I think that's important because if I push him too hard, it doesn't work. It has to come from him. So he chose, 'No, actually I want to go back to the Saturday school. This is better.' And now it's much easier."

And when Oliver is old enough, he will begin attending the Saturday school, too.

In fact, Izabela's work is directly connected to the whole network of Polish schools in the UK because she and her mother run a bookselling business that ships workbooks and other educational materials for use in these schools. At the same time, they also want to provide helpful resources for families seeking to raise bilingual children with Polish as the minority language.

Izabela mentioned, too, that she's also intent on reaching out to British schools in order to share some of the Polish language and culture in classrooms. "I think it's important that we start working with the British schools, too," she said. "I did that with my son's school and I had some really positive feedback about this, so I want to do more of it."

Such visits, she feels, could be beneficial to both the children with Polish backgrounds—like her own kids—and to the rest of the children as well. For children with Polish backgrounds, this sort of acknowledgement of the Polish language and culture within the school could help them feel welcome—particularly if they've moved to the UK from Poland—and view this part of their identity in a positive light. At the same time, she said, sharing the language and culture of different nations, like Poland, with the other children can create greater understanding and help counter some of society's "negative feelings about immigration and people from other countries."

Visits to Poland and Polish visitors

Along with these multiple sources of exposure to the Polish language and culture while in England, each summer the family also takes a two-week trip to Poland to see extended family and enjoy a holiday together. "I love going back to Poland," Izabela said. "It's really special. And when we go, I try to encourage the children to do some things on their own—like buying ice cream—so they can have those experiences."

Her desire to have her children gain some independence on these trips is tied to thoughts of their future and potential opportunities in Poland. "I don't know what they'll decide to do in the future," Izabela said, "but I want them to have that option. And if they do decide to spend some time there, then they'll be able to because they'll have the language ability."

Although the family isn't able to travel to Poland as often as they would like, they also welcome visits at their home by extended family from Poland, such as Tomasz's mother and sister, which provide further injections of the minority language and culture into their lives in the UK.

Accepting their majority language side

While Izabela is pleased with the progress that Adam and Oliver have made in the minority language, she also acknowledges feeling some frustration about the process of advancing that ability and having her children use it as actively as she would like. And, like many parents, she has mixed feelings about how far to act on this frustration. "I've noticed that it's easier for them to express themselves in English," she said. "They sometimes struggle to find the right words in Polish or sometimes it's just harder to say things because the grammar is more complicated. I know Polish is harder for them, but I try to explain that it's important to me, and that it's important for them, that they learn it. I try to encourage them."

That encouragement extends to her sons' choice of language when they're communicating with each another. Instead of insisting that the boys speak Polish, she pursues a softer approach, such as the use of praise and rewards for making greater efforts to use the minority language together. "There's a part of me that wants to say to them, 'Just speak Polish!' But I try to be a supportive parent. I don't think it's necessary to push them that hard. I do have to accept that so much of their reality is in English. There's only the limited part of the world here in our house that's in Polish and almost everything else is in English. I accept that and I understand that English is in their heads. So I think it would be wrong of me to force it, to say, 'Speak Polish all the time.' I don't want to push it too far."

Instilling pride in their heritage

When other parents ask Izabela for advice on fostering their children's minority language side, she tells them, "Don't think it's just going to happen. You have to put some effort into it. Use every opportunity and try to speak to your child in your language as much as you can. Yes, sometimes it's hard, but it's fun as well, and very rewarding. When we go back to Poland, my kids always speak Polish. And when your children are able to communicate with all the members of the family, on their own, it's so rewarding."

"As a parent," she added, "I don't want my children to be ashamed of where they come from. I'm not ashamed of it. Why should they be ashamed of it? I want them to be proud of who they are and language is also a part of that. So I want them to be proud of the fact that they can speak another language and also proud of the fact that their parents are Polish."

AFTERWORD: The dominance of the majority language in daily life is a challenging condition that every family—even families where both parents speak the minority language—must continuously navigate on their long journey. This is why, if children will be schooled in the majority language, it behooves parents to make the most of the early formative years to foster a firm and active foundation in the minority language prior to the start of primary school and the spike in majority language exposure that this brings. The hard reality is, parents are able to exert the most influence over their children's lives, including their language development, during those younger years. This doesn't mean that our influence ends at a particular point in childhood, but it's nevertheless true that that influence gradually wanes as our kids grow older and lead increasingly independent lives, heavily immersed in the majority language. Even though Izabela and Tomasz are able to fortify their own actions to support the minority language with additional opportunities involving extended family and the wider community, the majority language remains a dominating force in the children's days. In other words, despite the inherently higher odds of success based on the circumstances of their lives, their bilingual aim still requires mindful and proactive efforts on an ongoing basis in order to maximize their sons' progress in Polish over the years of childhood.

CONTACT & RESOURCES FOR IZABELA

✉ iolendzki@gmail.com

🌐 czytamimowiepopolsku.com/pl

f facebook.com/czytamimowiepopolsku

f facebook.com/izabela.olendzki

📷 @czytam_po_polsku

📖 *Podaruj dziecku szansę na dwujęzyczność* (Polish edition of *Maximize Your Child's Bilingual Ability*)

15

Progress Grows Over Time, From Failure to Failure

- ▶ Elena was born in the former Soviet Union and grew up there as well as in Sweden, Israel, and the United States, where she has lived since the age of 14. Bilingual in Russian and English, she is now in law school after working as a software developer.

- ▶ Her husband, Joseph, is a software developer and is a monolingual English speaker with some limited ability in Russian.

- ▶ They have two daughters: Maya, 10.6 years old, and Katie, 7.3 years old.

- ▶ Elena speaks Russian to her daughters and English to Joseph. The girls are also learning Spanish in school.

- ▶ The family now lives in northern California.

"No! I'll never need English!" Elena once told her parents when she was a child.

Elena was born in Moscow, to Russian parents, and grew up speaking Russian. Looking back at her childhood, she said, "I wasn't a language nerd. In fact, my parents made me take English classes with a tutor and I hated it with a passion. I think I was upset that I had to do this when I could be out playing with my friends. I don't know, I just didn't enjoy it. But my parents said that English will be useful one day and I'd better learn it."

When Elena was 10, the family left the Soviet Union and sought political asylum in Sweden. As their case moved through the court system, that first year she attended a school for children needing to learn Swedish, then the second year, after gaining ability in this language, she went to a regular Swedish school.

But their request for political asylum wasn't granted and the family was forced to move again when Elena was 12. "We went to Israel because my mom is Jewish. And there are so many immigrants that they have a whole system: they put you in a Hebrew class for four months, seven hours a day, and you come out and go straight into a normal school and you're okay."

But after learning Swedish, and then Hebrew, Elena and her family relocated again when she turned 14. She explained, "My parents didn't want to stay in Israel because there's a military draft and they didn't feel comfortable with the idea of their daughters serving in the military in a conflict. And they won the green card lottery so they decided to come to the United States."

Maintaining her mother tongue

I asked Elena about how her Russian was faring during those years, considering that the family's mother tongue had become the minority language through experiences of three successive majority languages, from Swedish to Hebrew and then to English. "My Russian was progressing, but it was hard. In Sweden, there was a point where my sister and I switched to Swedish. It was my parents' lightbulb moment, like they had to protect the Russian. Then in Israel, I found it very hard to read and it was very isolating. There was a huge Russian community there, so I started reading the more adult books in Russian. My Russian got better through reading."

However, her immersion in the English environment of the U.S., particularly as a teen leading a more independent life, meant that the Russian influence around her, and her own language ability, began to wane. "At some point, I just started being more comfortable in English and reading more in English," she said. "And when I went to college, I didn't have any Russian friends. That meant I was only speaking Russian to my mom for about half an hour every week or so. By the time I finished college, I could barely speak Russian. In my first year after college, my dad came to visit and he gave me a

Russian book. He said, 'Please read this.' And I said, 'Why?' And he said, 'Well, you'll like it, first of all. Second of all, you need to remember Russian so I would like you to read at least one book a year.' That was the deal we made."

She paused, then went on. "I didn't finish that book. I don't know why. I don't think it was particularly difficult, but it was just hard enough that it wasn't interesting, so I didn't finish it. I still didn't read until Maya was born, then I started speaking Russian and remembering more and reading more books that my dad recommended. Then it got better again. But I still don't think I speak at an adult level. I think I'm stuck as a 13 – or 14-year-old girl with some minor grammar mistakes."

Feeling alone and discouraged

By the time Maya was born, Elena's sister had already had a son and was speaking to him in Russian. "So it just kind of seemed normal," she said, referring to her own decision to speak Russian to Maya.

At first, however, Elena found that her Russian was "too weak" to use consistently and it took about six months for her to fully switch to this language. While Joseph doesn't have much ability in Russian, and he's unable to be a source of direct support for their daughters' progress in this language, Elena said that he was there alongside her during those first six months, encouraging her to persevere. "He's the reason my children speak Russian!" she said with a laugh.

Elena and Joseph met in the state of Iowa, a part of the U.S. where exposure to Russian out in the community was limited. And because her parents lived many states away, the opportunity for their additional input—times of immersion that lent a big boost to her bilingual aim—was limited, too. As a result, Elena felt largely alone in her quest and discouraged by the early results.

"It was frustrating for the longest time," she said, "because Maya spoke perfect English and she was very verbal, very expressive—but she wouldn't do it in Russian. Back then, I wasn't sure why and it felt like she was rejecting me. I still remember, we were taking a bath and I asked her, 'Why don't you speak Russian to me?' And she said, 'I can't.' And I said, 'Why not?' 'Well, I just can't.' And then I flashed back to all the sobbing conversations I had with my mom who told me to speak Russian and I was like, 'You don't care about my emotions! I have things to say!' And I remembered that 'I can't' feeling. It was at that point I understood that it's not me, it's her, and it's not really about rejection, it's about ability."

This realization led Elena to concentrate on nurturing Maya's ability by focusing more intently on the building blocks of language she needed to respond in Russian. "'Yes' and 'no,' that was the first thing. And then it was 'I want'—'I want this,' 'I want that.' That's like 50% of a toddler's vocabulary! This targeted input was helpful to me because it allowed me to focus on little pieces of it and not go crazy. I repeated these things a hundred times, and eventually she started saying them. And I was like, 'Yes! Okay, now the next thing, and keep the old thing,' so it builds into this momentum."

Since the bigger goal of bilingual fluency is a long-term effort, and can only be achieved at a gradual day-to-day pace, these smaller micro-goals enabled Elena to continue moving forward and gener-ating incremental progress. At the same time, she likened the larger process of promoting fluency to the idea of "filling a bucket" in the sense that once the bucket of language is full, and finally overflows, that language then naturally becomes more active. "The plan was to fill her up with Russian," she said, "so, eventually, it would come back out. I knew there was a point where you stop saying 'I can't' and you just express it, but that's after the point where you understand everything. So it's in there, but it's just not coming out yet."

Elena said that the situation slowly improved after that, with Maya using more and more Russian with her, but also admitted that "it wasn't the only time I was frustrated, because then she wouldn't read in Russian. There are a lot of things she prefers in English—all of them, in fact. And it's always like, 'Why not? We have good books in Russian. We have good stuff. Why not?' But I think I came to a moment of zen, where I decided that that's who she is. I can't really take away that part of her. But I can strengthen the other half, too."

The journey continues in California

Maya had just turned 5, and Katie was nearly 2, when the family moved from Iowa to California—where they abruptly had access to a much bigger Russian community and the many opportunities this brings for greater language exposure and engagement. In fact,

Katie was placed in Russian daycare and quickly became dominant in the minority language, even to the extent that Joseph had some difficulty understanding her until her English improved.

At the same time, Elena took the girls to play dates with Russian-speaking children and cultural activities like theater performances and holiday celebrations. She also enrolled Maya in a Russian school on Saturdays, but found that the school wasn't a good fit for Maya, as it was geared to children at a native level and employed a strict Russian learning style. "We did the Russian school for a year," Elena said, "but she just hated it. She liked the class, but the homework was a constant fight because they were teaching to a level she wasn't at yet. I felt like, yeah, she's getting Russian exposure but it's killing her self-esteem and she's starting to hate the language, so we stopped. On the other hand, the kids that are more like her, the second generation or kids from mixed families, they don't really speak Russian all that well, if at all. So she's in that gap right now."

Elena told me that, at this point, Maya speaks Russian to her "99% of the time. She has an occasional slip, especially when talking about school or about things she doesn't know the words for. Then she speaks Russian and fills in with English."

Katie, however—despite being dominant in the minority language when she was younger—now speaks more English than Russian. "She slips into English quite a bit even though she knows how to say it in Russian. There's this constant reminder, 'Speak Russian. Speak Russian.'"

Elena explained that Katie's bilingual ability began quickly tilting toward English once she entered an English-speaking school, two years ago. "Ever since, it's been a struggle to bring back Russian," she said. "Because of the Russian preschool, I think I was more relaxed about things. With Maya, I cut off all English: I would only read in Russian; I would only speak in Russian. With Katie, I still spoke only in Russian, but I would read in English and I would be okay with that. With Maya, I think she got used to having to work for it, but Katie didn't. So when it became hard, I don't think she knew how to work at it, and she didn't. It seems like Russian preschool was a good idea, but maybe without Russian preschool she would have been better at this point? I don't know."

Adding to the family's challenge is a third language, Spanish, which neither parent speaks well yet are keen to support throughout childhood alongside Russian and English. Both Maya and Katie have been attending a bilingual elementary school program since kindergarten and have made significant strides in acquiring Spanish, too. "The Russian helps them learn Spanish," Elena said, "which is a useful language in the United States. But it's hard now for Maya because the work is becoming more academic. She doesn't know some of the words and I can't always help her because I don't know the words myself."

Long-term success from short-term failures

Over the years, Elena has come to view her bilingual journey with her daughters in a broader way, noting that the success she has experienced with them to this point has actually been advanced through a long string of "failures." She said, "When I look at it from close up, day to day, everything I do seems to fail. Except for speaking to them, every single thing I've tried—the Russian school, getting them to read every day—has not worked. But these things still give them a little boost each time and carry them upwards, failure to failure."

She continued, "Every little thing helps a little bit—not as much as I expected—but there's a thing after that and a thing after that. And sometimes, they make a jump. They'll use a word that you didn't know they knew or they'll use some grammar that you never thought they'd be able to get and you're like, 'Oh, I remember you as a 4-year-old saying 'I want strawberries' and now you're saying something in perfect Russian.' So it's only looking at the long term that I see any sort of success and the short term is just trying to find the next thing that will fail and then the next thing after that."

Elena acknowledged that it took some time for her to grow into this larger view of the girls' progress without feeling frustrated by what she considered failed efforts. "I've learned to live with it," she said. "It bothered me, initially, when things didn't work. But now I just go in knowing that this isn't forever, this is just the next thing to try. If it sticks, good, but if it doesn't stick, there's always another thing."

In this spirit, she advises, "Parents have to try a lot of things that won't work. But I think this can be very hard for people, like they hope to get a book that will tell them, 'Day one, do this. Day two, do that. Success guaranteed.' And it doesn't work like that because the circumstances for each family are so different. You have to try everything, and then some, to find the things that work for you. I think it's very hard for people to allow themselves to make their own mistakes and not get discouraged by them."

A broader view of being a bilingual family

"I think the other big thing that helped me be successful," Elena said, "is that I had to realize that the culture we have is not necessarily Russian. The culture we have is a bilingual family. And so you don't even need another Russian bilingual family. You just need another bilingual family—an environment where bilingual children are the norm. And this is where the Spanish school has helped us so much." She then explained how being part of a school where bilingual kids are the norm—kids from a range of nationalities and languages—has made her own children feel proud of their Russian side.

"Kids come up to them and say, 'You know Russian? That's so cool!' So it becomes this cool factor. And I think making a child feel comfortable actually goes a long way because that was my English experience when I was little. I was frustrated that I had to do this thing that other children didn't have to do. I remember when Maya was talking about a play date with one of her friends. Maya said, 'Oh, I can't do Saturdays. That's Russian school.' And this girl looked at her and said, 'Oh yeah, I can't do Saturdays, either, that's Korean school.' It's true, Maya doesn't speak Korean, but just that affirmative feedback, that 'Hey, I do this, too.' So the multicultural environment has helped her where just a pure Russian environment has sometimes been harsh."

Elena's broader view of her family as a bilingual family, not strictly a Russian bilingual family, also informs her outlook on bilingualism itself. "When people talk about bilingual children, it's a very schizophrenic sort of view. It's like, 'Oh, this is English Maya. This is Russian Maya. This is Spanish Maya.' But as a bilingual—as a balanced bilingual—there's just you. And you know, you might be more polite in cultures where people are more polite and you might be more aggressive in cultures where people are more aggressive. But your feelings, internally, are the same. It's not that you're different; it's just that you express these aspects of yourself in different ways."

She went on, "And I think it can be very harmful to split a child into two without fully respecting the other side. That's actually one of the better things my parents did for me: they respected the other me, the majority language me. I was allowed to have the books I wanted to have. I was allowed to do the things I wanted to do. It's just that they advertised the minority language side while respecting who I was. There was a moment when I hated Maya's English side. I was like, 'Why, child? I want Russian Maya.' And then I realized that there is no Russian Maya and there is no English Maya—it's one Maya and the sooner I learn to respect all of her, the better."

AFTERWORD: Elena's thoughtful reflections on her experience—particularly when it comes to coping with setbacks and frustrations—underscore the central idea that success at raising a bilingual child involves our psychological and emotional mindset as much as it does our knowledge and technique. Her wise perspective on "failure" conveys the crucial point that parents needn't pursue this quest perfectly in order to achieve significant success over time. In fact, such success can be realized even through endless failures—as long as these "failures" continue from day to day over the full length of the childhood years. Thus, the only way to truly fail at the greater, long-term goal is to give up entirely somewhere along the way due to discouragement over short-term setbacks and frustrations. If you simply persevere in your efforts, as Elena's example demonstrates, you *will* succeed to some rewarding degree. In my experience, parents sometimes "get in their own way" by "overthinking" their difficulties. Yes, it's important to give strategic thought to our actions and the results they produce so that these actions can be as effective as possible. That's a positive way to address difficulties. But if we "overthink" things, we may cross the line into a negative state of mind, with feelings of disappointment and doubt becoming obstacles to further efforts and greater progress. So the constructive notion of "failing upward," as Elena suggested, means accepting that your experience will inevitably be imperfect—as it is for us all—and yet you pledge to yourself to simply continue moving forward and trying again, then again and again, while reaching out for support from others, as needed. This is the sort of productive mindset that will help make your journey both more joyful and more successful.

16

Non-native Speaker Keeps Up Efforts at Home and Abroad

▶ Michele is American and lives in the U.S. with her husband and their four children. She is a non-native speaker of French and blogs about her experience at the site Intentional Mama (intentionalmama.com).

▶ Her husband, Anouxa, is originally from Thailand. He came to the U.S. at the age of 4. He speaks English, Thai, and Lao. He and Michele are both teachers.

▶ Their children are Sophia, 10.9 years old; Ethan, 7.11 years old; Nolan, 4.11 years old; and Elliot, 1.9 years old.

▶ Michele speaks French to the children, Anouxa speaks English to them (and a bit of Lao), and the couple communicates in English.

▶ The family lives in a small town in the U.S. state of Oregon.

"It's kind of amusing," Michele said with a laugh, "that my husband grew up bilingual and I didn't, and yet I'm now the one raising our children to be bilingual."

Michele, who was born in the U.S., was a monolingual child, raised in English. In primary school, she was told that her maiden name had come down from her father's great-grandparents, who were French speakers living in Canada but were believed to have been originally from France. This information sparked an early interest in this heritage, and, as a fifth grader, she chose France when asked to prepare a report about one of the world's nations. But her first taste of the French language did not come until she was in high school.

"It wasn't until tenth grade that I could choose to take a language and I chose French," Michele said. "That was really the first time I had heard French, when I went into the French classroom. I loved it! I don't think it particularly came naturally or easily to me, but because I loved it, it was a joy for me."

Michele took three years of French in high school and, though she started as a pre-med student in college, she continued studying French, too. When she was 20, she studied abroad in France for one semester—her first time in a French-speaking country—and that experience, spending time with other exchange students from a range of countries, changed her career path.

"It was so fascinating," she explained. "I thought, 'You know, I think I want to teach English to exchange students or other English language learners.' So I went into teaching because of that experience living in France. I came back and spent one year in a Master's in Teaching program, which is where I met my husband."

Speaking French to her firstborn

While Michele was born in the U.S., Anouxa was born in Thailand in an area bordering Laos. Before his family immigrated to the U.S., when he was 4, he spoke no English. His mother was Lao and his father was Thai and the family spoke mainly in Lao. Anouxa learned English quickly after arriving in the U.S. yet the family maintained their communication in Lao as he was growing up. Michele said that, although he now mixes a lot of English into his Lao, he continues to use it with his parents and extended family members.

"We met when I was 21, and we dated for a while," she said. "I taught French for the first few years after we met."

Though Michele had originally been intent on teaching English to English language learners, it turned out that the teaching program she entered did not enable her to specialize in this area. But during her experience of student teaching, she enjoyed spending time with the French teacher at that school and decided to obtain an endorsement for teaching French, too.

"So I did teach French for a little bit and then I thought, 'If I'm going to be teaching French, I would love to gain more fluency.' So when I was 24, I went back to France as a study abroad student, this time for a full school year, and I loved it."

After returning to the U.S., Michele resumed teaching French, and she and Anouxa got married. "Two years later," she said, "our daughter came along and I thought, 'You know, I've seen how hard it is for my middle school and high school students to learn a language, and I might as well just try speaking French with my own child and maybe by the time she's 2 or 3, I'll have to switch back to English because I'm not a native speaker, but at least I can try. So that's how our bilingual family journey began."

Less exposure to Lao

At the same time, Anouxa did not feel the same drive to speak Lao to their first child. "I think that's because he was just far more comfortable in English," Michele explained. "He'd probably spent most of his life trying to integrate and be seen as an American, and he didn't see a need for our children to speak Thai or Lao."

Michele respected his decision, though she thinks that Anouxa came to feel some regret over not exposing the children to more Lao, especially when their daughter, at 7 or 8, wondered aloud why she couldn't speak Lao like his side of the family.

"With each child," Michele said, "I kind of hinted that, 'Hey, you can speak Lao with this one!' Because you really do get another chance at it when you're starting at the beginning, and we've had four children. So my husband does use some Lao words or phrases with our youngest, who's now 20 months old, a toddler. He'll even tell me, 'Hey, I'm teaching him some Lao!', but it's not a concerted 100% effort where we're trying to raise him in this language, too."

Strengthening her own French

Looking back at the beginning of her own aim to use French with their firstborn, Sophia, Michele admits that it took a few months for her to become accustomed to using French consistently when speaking to her. Then, as Sophia grew older, Michele felt challenged by shortcomings in her own French ability.

"I remember just the most basic things seemed a little hard to say, like 'pull the plug in the bathtub and let the bathwater out.' There were things I didn't know how to say and so I'd look them up, like how to say 'plug.' But babies don't care, toddlers don't care, and so I'd test it out and start using the new word myself."

Michele pointed to two things that were particularly helpful for advancing her own fluency in the target language at that time: a dictionary app for her smartphone and a subscription service, called Les Petits Livres, that sends French children's books by mail.

She explained, "They'd send me four books each month and I'd mail them back. Reading children's books, there was a lot of basic vocabulary and grammar. Little by little, as my daughter's French was developing, I was also improving my own fluency. That was a nice benefit that I didn't foresee: not only could I teach her what I already knew, I would actually learn quite a bit more over the years."

While Michele was thrilled with the early progress that Sophia was making in French, she also recognized, early on, that her own efforts alone would not be sufficient for her bilingual aim.

"It was really fun to see her language development. Her first words were French, like 'avi' for 'avion' ('airplane'). It was really cute to see those French words coming out. But I think I could also see, in her toddler years, that my influence was not enough. She was speaking some French phrases, but also some English phrases, and you could see that it was starting to tip—maybe at around 2 and a half to 3 years old—towards English."

Empowering actions and reflections

At that point, Michele began seeking out other French speakers and settings in order to fortify her daughter's language input. She made long drives to take Sophia to a weekly children's French class at the nearest Alliance Française (an international organization that promotes the French language and francophone culture) and to meetings, every couple of months, of families wanting French exposure for their kids. Although the outside support she was able to access was limited, she feels it was fruitful, and also in the sense that making these efforts helped strengthen her own commitment to her bilingual aim. After all, extra efforts like this—like driving an hour or two for a modest, but beneficial, amount of language exposure—demonstrates the degree of importance we attach to this goal.

It was around that time, too, that Michele began blogging at the thoughtful site she named Intentional Mama. Asked what sort of impact writing about her experience has had on her efforts and her success, she replied, "It's been instrumental, I think, in shaping my identity for myself as a parent who is really committed to bilingualism and raising my kids bilingually, in French and English. I would say that having the blog has been very helpful in helping me remember that this is a high priority, if not among the highest priorities, in raising our children."

Meanwhile, Michele has also sought to bring French speakers into their home for extended periods of time: a homestay guest, an exchange student, even an au pair to contribute to her children's language development and cultural awareness. Overall, she feels that these opportunities have been very positive, though in some cases their visitors were more introverted than she had anticipated. She recommends that, whenever possible, parents try to host minority language speakers who are naturally extroverted and will talk a lot with the children.

Enriching trips to France

Michele has been very proactive about providing her children with as much input in French as possible, though she admits that this can be quite challenging when you yourself are largely the sole source of the minority language. It was this feeling, along with the fact that her daughter's English was becoming more dominant, that led her to consider taking a trip to France so the children could gain a full-on immersion experience of the language and culture. Because she and Anouxa are teachers, with long summer breaks, the family could potentially travel during that time.

"And I thought," she said, "if we're going to spend time in France, we should probably stay as long as possible. If we're paying for the airfare, we want to get as much time out of it as we can."

As Michele continued to explore this idea, she discovered that other parents had not only taken their kids to a minority language destination, they had been able to have their children attend school there for a short period of time.

"I thought, well, we could go in summer and I could stay longer with the kids and enroll them in school. I had no idea if that was really possible, but I thought, let's just try—and we were able to pull it off!"

It turned out that the children were able to spend five weeks in the French school before Michele had to bring them home to the U.S. (and to Anouxa, who had returned earlier). "It was fantastic," she said, "but it felt like it wasn't long enough. We were just starting to make friends, we were just getting integrated, and then it was time to go."

Because that first trip proved to be such an exciting and enriching experience, the family then returned to France for a second visit—and were able to have the children attend school for seven weeks this time. They are now contemplating a third trip...or even the idea of living abroad for a year or two.

Gaining fluency in French

Asked about her children's progress in French to this point, particularly the two elder kids, Michele said, "My daughter is very fluent and I'm very proud of her. It's really rewarding to me, as a parent, when we're in France and I meet another parent at school and I tell them a little about our story and they can see that I have a slight accent or I'm not a native speaker. And then my daughter will come out of class and say something to me and the French person—this has happened a couple of times—will turn to me with this look of astonishment and say, 'But she has no accent!' They're just floored that her French is so good."

Her eldest son, too, has made satisfying progress, though Michele said that Ethan is more of an introvert and that difference in personality makes him a less active speaker than Sophia. "He doesn't reply as much in French to me," Michele said, "but he's still capable. In fact, just the other day, he was watching TV with my husband, my husband's brothers, and our exchange student. Apparently, Ethan and our exchange student were having a conversation in French and my husband told me that his brothers were amazed because they hadn't realized he was that fluent in French!"

Making the experience joyful

When Michele offers advice to other parents—whether native speakers of the minority language or non-native speakers like herself—she stresses the importance of "bringing joy into it" by attaching the target language to enjoyable experiences. "For example, you always play a certain game in Spanish, or when you eat this dessert at lunchtime you play this French song. So you start making these associations that are positive and joyful and fun and then I don't think you're going to get that feedback of 'Mommy, this is weird and hard.'"

At the same time, Michele pointed to the less pleasant but unavoidable fact that money is also an important consideration when it comes to fueling progress on the bilingual journey. "A part of this is financial," she said. "There are always financial concerns like, 'Oh, maybe we don't need to take a trip this year' or 'Maybe we shouldn't be subscribing to this every month,' but I don't think we ever look back and say, 'It wasn't worth the cost.' When you get to the goal—when your children are speaking fluently—you don't look back and regret the expense. So I think we just have to get over that factor and be consistent in realizing that the goal is worth it."

AFTERWORD: Over the years I've shared a number of guest posts at Bilingual Monkeys on the theme of "Bilingual Travelers." These personal reflections by parents—which include an article by Michele detailing her family's first trip to France—vividly illustrate the tremendous power of trips to minority language locations. Such experiences of immersion in the target language and culture often give a significant boost to a family's bilingual aim, enabling the children to leap forward in their language development and cultural understanding. As Michele's story shows, when travel experiences are added to daily, ongoing efforts at home, the combined effect can produce very rewarding progress. Of course, the idea of traveling to a minority language destination may be daunting, but if this is at all possible for your family, it could be well worth the energy and investment. While my own family's trips from Japan to the U.S. have been limited, which means my kids have spent only a total of a few weeks of their lives there, I still couldn't agree more with Michele's view that, looking back, our travels were clearly worth it. In fact, they were priceless experiences for the whole family, and in a way that went beyond language and culture. In our case, as is true for many bilingual families, such trips are practically the only way for children to spend time, in person, with grandparents and other family members. Now that my kids are older, and their grandparents are gone, I feel glad and grateful that we pursued the trips that we did manage to take.

CONTACT & RESOURCES FOR MICHELE

✉ michelecherie@hotmail.com

🌐 intentionalmama.com

f facebook.com/intentionalmama

17

Building Community and Boosting the Success of Many Families

- ▶ Marta is originally from Spain. Along with her native language, she speaks German and English. She is an electrical engineer, but is currently taking time off from her career.

- ▶ Her husband, Jens, is German. A researcher in the field of medical technology, he is multilingual in German, Spanish, and English.

- ▶ They live in Germany with their three children: Carlos, 10.11 years old; Alba, 7.5 years old; and Diego, 4.6 years old.

- ▶ Currently, Marta speaks only Spanish with the children while Jens and the kids communicate in both German and Spanish.

Growing up in Spain, Marta began acquiring English from a young age. Every summer, from the age of 9 through her time as a university student, she took part in various activities that fueled her development in this language: summer camps in English, homestays in Ireland, study abroad and work abroad opportunities in the U.S. "From 16 onwards," she said, "I felt I could speak English well. And I could read books in English without any problems."

When she was 20, she started to learn German by attending a language course on the weekend. Then, in her last year of college, she came to Germany as part of the Erasmus program, which enables European students to spend a year studying in another European country.

She met Jens at her university in Germany.

"When we first met," Jens said, "I hardly knew any Spanish. Then shortly after, I decided to study abroad in Spain. I had to improve my Spanish and Marta wanted to improve her German. So we met several times, with only that in mind, to improve our languages. But it ended up being an intensive course that changed both of our lives!"

"I then went back to Spain for a year," Marta said. "And then I moved to Germany. So I've been living here since 2001."

Jens acknowledged that, in his youth, he had been far more interested in sports than in languages. "I was good at school, especially subjects like mathematics and physics, but in languages, I was only average. So back then, I don't think I even liked languages very much."

However, his decision to transfer to the university where he met Marta, in the middle of his college years, led to an "eye-opening experience." Alongside his relationship with Marta, he developed friendships with other international students, including many students from Spain. "My strategy was to just hang out with them and go to their parties and other activities. Of course, with each other they were only speaking Spanish and I would listen in, but all of them understood German, too, so I could answer in German. And that made it much easier for me at the beginning. So I actually learned Spanish, not so much from textbooks, but by going to parties with all the Spanish people!"

By the time of their wedding—which included guests from 16 countries—Marta and Jens were clearly on a path where their children would be raised in an international spirit while following in their own trilingual footsteps.

Language use, resources, and visitors

Since Spanish is the family's main minority language, Marta and Jens have long been proactive about providing ample exposure for this language, both in and out of the home. From the very start of their trilingual journey, Marta has been very consistent about using Spanish with the kids. "I always talk to the children in Spanish," she said. "What I find challenging, though, is when we're with people who don't speak Spanish. So what I do is, I say whatever I have to say in both languages. If it's just for my child, I say it only in Spanish. But if I'm talking to the group, like 'Okay, wash your hands. We're eating now,' then I say it in both languages, Spanish and German."

Jens noted that Marta's persistence in using Spanish—even when out in public—has been one of the keys to their family's success. At the same time, his own ability in Spanish is an important source of support for Marta's efforts. "At the beginning," he said, "we made it really separate so she was speaking strictly Spanish and I was speaking strictly German. But then we noticed that, for the majority language, it's not so important for us to be consistent because the children are getting enough German exposure, anyhow."

At this point, then, while Marta remains consistent in her use of the minority language—and uses a limited amount of German to include those who don't understand Spanish—Jens has come to speak both languages more freely with the kids. "With Jens, they feel at ease talking in both languages," Marta said.

"Yeah, it feels normal," Jens agreed.

"But I don't think it feels normal for them to talk to me in German," Marta said.

Along with this input from the speech of both parents, Marta has also been diligent about enriching their home with resources. "I try to have as many materials in Spanish as I can," she said. "They don't watch German TV. They only watch TV or DVDs in Spanish. We don't have many German books, either. We get German books from the library and I buy a lot of Spanish books. We have a very big Spanish library."

"I always say we have the biggest library of Spanish kids' books in this part of the country," Jens said with a laugh.

Visitors, too, often Spanish or English speakers, are regular sources of input and inspiration for the children. "We've always liked having guests at our house," Marta said. "But since we have kids, it's become more important. When we hear someone is coming to the area, we tell them, 'Stay at our place! We have enough room!' For example, last year, for the whole month of December, we had people staying here."

"We never went below nine people in this house!" Jens added.

Marta admitted that hosting visitors can also be tiring, but both of them agreed that these experiences are still well worth the effort not only for the contributions they make to the children's language ability and lives, but also for the sheer enjoyment they bring to the whole family and their guests.

Creating a minority language community

Outside the home as well, they have been able to take advantage of local opportunities to engage their children in Spanish—or even create new opportunities for themselves and other Spanish-speaking families. The municipal government maintains a program of Spanish classes for native Spanish-speaking children, which all three kids have been attending, while the oldest, Carlos, is now at a middle school which has a strong program in language learning, including Spanish and English.

At the same time, Marta has been extremely proactive about *creating community*. When Carlos was 18 months old, she reached out to friends with kids of around the same age and formed a play group for Spanish-speaking parents and their children. Though it began as a small group for small children that met at her house, it has grown over the years and continues to meet weekly—in large rented rooms in the city's Red Cross building—more than a decade later. Today, in fact, the play group welcomes families with young children of all ages to engage in indoor activities in Spanish and has even produced a spin-off group—a sports group—that meets at a different time for outdoor fun.

However, as Marta noted, while the meetings of the group are intended to be playful gatherings, she has also had to be firm about maintaining the basic purpose of the group as a "monolingual" domain for its members. "We have the rule that you have to speak Spanish," she said. "So the children have to have Spanish at home. Sometimes there are people with children who are learning Spanish at home and they want to come into the group, but I have to be strict. I have to play the bad cop and tell them, 'I'm sorry, but this group isn't for your child.' I explain that, in the group, they have to speak Spanish all the time because this is the only place where our children can hear only Spanish. So no German is allowed. The children need to speak Spanish."

"If there's any German," Jens said, "there's a danger of having a breakout of German during that special hour of the week and then it becomes pointless."

"I think they should understand that this isn't a Spanish school," Marta continued. "Because otherwise, it doesn't make any sense. It breaks all the effort."

Marta's efforts to create community have also expanded beyond the play group itself by organizing special Spanish activities and events for families from the group and other Spanish-speaking families in the area. Over the years she has helped spearhead a variety of fun gatherings that have brought the same kind of benefits as the play group to all the participants. These activities and events have included barbecues, storytelling shows, music classes, guided tours of the city and surrounding nature, screenings of Spanish movies at a local cinema, a festival of the world's Spanish-speaking countries, and even an annual Christmas event on an old steam train. "There's a Christmas train in December," Marta said, "and we reserve one big wagon for the Spanish community. Then we go together and sing Spanish carols and Saint Nicholas comes on the train and gives all the kids little gifts. It's become a tradition that we do every year."

Of course, there's also the more trying side to creating community. Organizing a play group or a special activity or event—as with hosting visitors in your home—requires a commitment of time and energy. Yet the payoff, as Marta's story shows, can be enormously rewarding for so many. This is why, she explained, her eyes are always open to fresh possibilities for creating community, and she pursues new ideas "whenever I see someone who can do something in Spanish!"

Spending regular time in Spain, too

On top of all the productive efforts Marta and Jens are making in Germany to support their children's Spanish side, regular trips to Spain are a central part of their lifestyle, too. Taking advantage of the proximity between the two countries, "we try to go to Spain as often as we can," Marta said.

"That's four times a year, for at least a week," Jens said. "But sometimes even two weeks. I think we're very lucky. Marta's parents can easily accommodate us so it's really a pleasure to be there." He added how fortunate he was that his company allows him to do his work remotely from Spain for a few days each year so that, combined with his vacation time, he's able to join Marta and the kids on every trip.

"And when we come back to Germany," Marta said. "I always notice that their Spanish is stronger. Now and then they ask me, 'Why do I have to speak in Spanish to you if you also understand German?' But I always tell them, 'In Spain, all of our family and friends don't speak German. If you don't use your Spanish every day, you'll forget it and then you won't be able to talk to them.' And since they all love going to Spain, this is a big motivation for them."

Jens continued, "So usually three out of four times a year, we go to see the family and then it's clear to the kids that they have to speak Spanish to have a good time with them. Then the fourth time we go to a big summer camp that Marta's parents have been going to for almost 40 years, which has grown into a group of newborns to senior citizens. And at this camp there are peers in every age group so the children have a lot of Spanish-speaking friends of the same age. This is also very important for making the point that Spanish is relevant for them."

"And when they come home from the summer camp," Marta said, "their Spanish is better because they talk like children their age. Otherwise, they're learning mostly from me and, since I'm a grown-up, I don't speak the slang that children speak."

She went on to emphasize that the immersion of these camp vacations not only advances the children's language development, it also deepens their connection to the Spanish culture. "For example, this summer they learned a lot of jokes and they're now telling them all the time. They also learn the songs that the Spanish people sing and how the culture works, how they greet each other, how they have fun. So it's the language, but it's much more than that, too."

Staying resourceful to address challenges

While the family has clearly experienced a lot of rewarding success on their journey to date—and will no doubt experience similar success with English in the future—this doesn't mean that Marta and Jens have no concerns regarding the road ahead. Even the most successful parents face certain challenges that they must navigate as effectively as they can in order to maximize their children's language development.

"I'm happy with their progress," Marta said. "The one that worries me, though, is Alba because I see, from her personality, that she's a very social child. She always wants to be with friends and 99% of the time these are German-speaking friends. On the other hand, her social skills are an advantage in Spain because she's also social in Spain. But, of course, the majority of the time, we're here. And she's not very keen on reading, either. So the Spanish in her life is much less than Carlos and Diego. Maybe later she'll develop an interest in books, I don't know. But I can see that she's different and I need to find other strategies that appeal to her."

Marta's words underscore the importance of matching our efforts, as effectively as we can, with the personalities and interests of each child. At the same time, these efforts will naturally need to evolve as our children grow. "The thing is with children," she said, "they change. You have your routines and things, and then the child changes and you have to adapt. So I think that as a parent, not only with languages but with everything, you have to keep being creative and ask yourself: 'What can I do?'"

An inspiring example of success

This key question is clearly in the forefront of Marta's mind, from day to day, and continues to drive her ongoing efforts. A good example of this took place at the last summer camp in Spain when she asked the Spanish children what their favorite books and movies were in order to come up with fresh resources for her own kids. "You always have to have new inspiration," she said. "So I made a list of all the books and films."

Marta's proactive nature, combined with her children's strong bilingual ability, has made her a role model for other families with a bilingual aim. Her actions not only fuel her own family's progress, the example of their success, along with the opportunities and advice she offers to others, is helping to inspire greater progress among other families, too.

"Sometimes it's hard," she said. "Sometimes it feels like a lot of effort for a little result. But every little thing you do counts. And keep asking yourself: 'Why is it worth it? Why is this important to me?' For me, my main motivation is that my children can talk to my family and that, if they want, they can go to my country and feel at home."

"I think it's very helpful to look for people with the same goal," Jens said, "because you can put the efforts on many people's shoulders. The other big strategy is to combine what you like with what is useful. For example, Marta likes reading books, so for her, it's a lot of fun to read aloud to them every evening for a full hour or longer, in her language. So you do fun things that you really like, and they really like, and that also serve your purpose."

"If you do it like a school environment where they're just sitting and learning, it's harder," Marta said. "I was thinking, if Diego doesn't want to go to the play group on Wednesdays, 'Okay, what do I do?' I have my Plan B. If he doesn't want to go, I could invite two families from the group that have children of Diego's age, and we could do things together at home, maybe not every week, but every couple of weeks. I was thinking, what's the most important thing that Diego gets from the play group? And for me, it's friends that speak Spanish, friends from Spanish-speaking families."

Marta paused, and smiled. "He likes the play group now so the problem is solved. But I told the other moms, 'We can do it anyway!'"

AFTERWORD: I was fortunate to get a first-hand look at the impressive power of creating community when I paid a visit to Marta and her family and tagged along for a meeting of her long-running minority language play group. In all, there were about 30 parents and children in attendance, separated into two rooms by age and involved in playful activities that both the parents and their kids were clearly enjoying. While I was there for only that one afternoon, to think that this play group has been actively meeting, week after week, *for years* makes the group a shining example of how initiative and persistence can produce tremendous benefits for so many families: in language development, cultural understanding, mutual support, and friendship. In fact, this influence, as Marta noted, extends to families of other minority languages, too, and even monolingual families, inspiring them to enhance their own experiences of languages and cultures.

From a bird's-eye view, gazing down on humanity as a whole, this also means that more bridges are being built between more people. "I think we bilingual families are not only influencing our kids and their lives," she said, "but also making a more tolerant and open world for other people around us." Thus, our own efforts to raise bilingual kids can end up radiating out into the world much farther than we might ever imagine from the first small steps we take. The truth is, these efforts can even impact the world itself.

CONTACT & RESOURCES FOR MARTA

✉ kikirime@gmail.com

🌐 kikiricosas.blogspot.com

18

Creative Projects Promote Language Use and Greater Progress

- ▶ Nellie is originally from Hungary and now lives in the countryside in the U.S. state of Missouri. She is multilingual, with proficiency in Hungarian, English, and Japanese, and works as a freelance translator and proofreader. She also serves as the coordinator for an area association of organic food growers and, with her kids, regularly helps at a local orchard.

- ▶ Her husband, Scott, is American and speaks English; his ability in Hungarian is limited. He works as a water plant operator for their small city.

- ▶ The couple has two children: a daughter, Zita, 11.1 years old, and a son, Zalán, 8.3 years old, who are being homeschooled.

In the same spirit as the podcast pursued by Deepti, and the album of children's music created by Ana, Nellie has put substantial effort into creative projects that involve her family's minority language. The examples of these three parents demonstrate that, beyond the essential daily language exposure generated through ample speech and reading aloud, such projects can engage children in additional activities that further their use of the target language, fortify their interest in the language itself, and facilitate other kinds of learning about the world.

Though creative projects of various kinds and sizes are often a productive part of the success stories of many families, Nellie's efforts are particularly noteworthy in their scale and influence. The projects that she has undertaken have not only helped empower her own family's bilingual journey, they serve as a source of ideas and inspiration for other families as well.

A multilingual, multicultural direction

Nellie was born and raised in Hungary, so Hungarian is her first language. She started learning English and Japanese in elementary school and then, in junior high school, began studying German and Latin, too. "These were my languages when I graduated from high school," she said, "but they weren't all at the same level."

In college she was a double major in Cognitive Psychology and Japanese Linguistics. Referring to her efforts to learn Japanese, she said, "I had put so much work into it that I decided I didn't want to give it up. That's why I majored in Japanese along with Psychology."

Meanwhile, as a junior in high school, she was a foreign exchange student in the U.S. and then, as a college student, began spending her summers working at summer camps there. It was at one of these summer camps that she met Scott. After a few more years traveling between Hungary, the U.S., and Japan, Nellie finally settled in the U.S. for good, where she and Scott got married and the couple welcomed their two children.

What motivates her bilingual aim

"To tell you the truth," Nellie explained, when I asked about making plans to raise their kids bilingually, "the first baby I ever held in my hands was my own. I didn't have little cousins. I didn't have family nearby, so I didn't know what I was doing. We knew we wanted to start a family, but we didn't really have plans. My parents don't speak English at all, though, and I wanted my kids to have a connection with them. That was the main motivator. I wanted them to be able to communicate with their grandparents."

"I had a hidden motive, too," she continued. "When I'm 85 and they're 60 and I want a glass of water but I don't speak my second language anymore because I'm losing this ability, I want to make sure that somebody understands me!"

Nellie shared that she had initially hoped Scott would gain some ability in Hungarian in order to develop a deeper understanding of the culture. But despite several attempts over the years, this hope hasn't been realized. "His personality makes it possible for him to communicate with anybody in English, even if they don't speak English," she said. "He's just so outgoing and social. He uses his arms to explain everything, so there was never any real need for him to learn."

She then offered the example of Scott and her father gesturing back and forth to somehow convey the various models of cars that they've owned and what they thought about those vehicles. "It was surprisingly accurate," she said of their communication, "despite my father not speaking any English and my husband not speaking any Hungarian."

Fostering active use of the minority language

Since Scott lacks ability in Hungarian, Nellie, like many minority language parents, must use the majority language to communicate with her partner. Nellie's use of English, though, isn't limited to Scott because she also uses English when the whole family is together and often speaks English to the children, too.

For many families in similar circumstances, where the minority language parent is also freely using the majority language, this scenario can undercut the two core conditions of exposure and need to such a significant degree that the children may grow to have only passive ability in that language. Nellie and her kids, however, are overcoming the odds and experiencing considerable success. While she acknowledges that "their native language is definitely English and Hungarian is a second language," Zita and Zalán are nevertheless now active speakers of the minority language as a result of a number of productive actions she has pursued over the years.

VIDEO CALLS WITH GRANDPARENTS

While many families make regular video calls with extended family members, Nellie has maintained these calls as *a daily routine*. Every morning, from 7:30 to 8:00, they speak to her parents in Hungarian, which provides a concentrated time of exposure and need for the minority language. Since her parents don't speak English, the kids have a natural need to use Hungarian. Although Zalán is not yet as proficient as Zita, he can still converse with them on his own. To encourage this, Nellie often asks him to start the Skype call himself. "I tell him to go ahead and call and I leave him there for a few minutes," she said. "And he's able to communicate without a problem. But as soon as I'm in the room, it's just more convenient for him to sit back, thinking, 'Oh, Mommy will tell them what's going on.'"

HOMESCHOOLING

Meanwhile, Nellie is homeschooling them in both languages, which means they receive daily exposure to Hungarian in this way, too, including reading and writing activities. "And every 12 weeks," she said, "we have a topic that we all do together. We've done family finances, geography, archaeology, and that's been about 80% in Hungarian." Nellie added that she doesn't "force" the children to stay in Hungarian during their schoolwork, instead relying on the task itself to motivate their use of the language. "The task is given in Hungarian in their books, but if they have questions, I don't mind discussing it in English or a mix of the two languages, then they respond in Hungarian in the workbook."

MUSIC

"Music has played a more important part in their Hungarian language development than I would have thought," Nellie said. "I was always a horrible music student. I can't sing for anything. But all the kids' songs I knew were in Hungarian and my parents supplied the CDs so for many years, every time we get in the car—and in America, we spend a lot of time in the car—it's 'Mommy, can you turn on the music?' So now Zita is playing Hungarian folk songs on her violin and that's what she's singing. And Zalán picks up on all of it because he's listening to Zita sing. With the lyrics, they pick up a lot of vocabulary—a lot of Hungarian that I otherwise wouldn't have been able to teach them because you just don't use those words in everyday speech."

VISITS TO HUNGARY

Short trips to Hungary, of two or three weeks, have also been a very productive part of the family's bilingual journey. To date, Zita has been to Hungary six times and Zalán has been there four times and each of these immersion experiences enables the children to make impressive leaps forward in their use of the minority language. "It's amazing when we go there because, in less than 24 hours, Zalán switches completely to Hungarian, too," Nellie said. "And when we're Skyping with Scott from Hungary, Zalán sometimes starts speaking to Scott in Hungarian! Their ability to just land there and start speaking the language and communicating at a much higher level very quickly, compared to what they produce when they're here, it's just amazing."

Creative projects promote progress, too

AROUND THE WORLD WITH ALFONZO

When Zita was 6 and Zalán was 3, Nellie hit upon her "first crazy idea," as she put it, for a creative project. "I wanted to do something that would connect them to the rest of the world," she said, "something that would show them how big the world is."

Over the course of a year, Nellie and her kids followed the adventures of a stuffed animal—a friendly-looking alligator named Alfonzo—on a worldwide journey as he traveled to eight countries and visited 12 families for homestays. Moving by post from place to place, Alfonzo was welcomed by each family, who sent messages back to Nellie and her kids, in Alfonzo's voice, and took photos of his local "experiences."

In most countries, the messages that the families sent, as well as the responses made by Zita and Zalán, were written in English, then Nellie and the kids translated everything into Hungarian. When Alfonzo stayed in Hungary with several families, the letters arrived in Hungarian, and these were translated into English. The messages and photos were posted online at two websites Nellie maintained, one in English and one in Hungarian, in order to share Alfonzo's adventures with the world.

Though Nellie sustained these parallel sites until the end of the project when Alfonzo finally returned home, after the first six months it became difficult to keep up the children's interest in the translation work and so Nellie took over this task herself. She pointed to the fact that the English site generated a more enthusiastic response than the Hungarian site and so the value of the translation work, in the children's eyes, diminished over time.

Still, this captivating project not only effectively engaged Zita and Zalán in their two languages, it proved to be rewarding in other ways, too—rewards that continue to reverberate today. As she had originally hoped, "it expanded their view of the world," she said. "And it's still having an effect. Five years later, we're still making crepes based on the recipe that they sent us from France! Often when a country or city comes up in conversations, they'll ask, 'Is that where Alfonzo had his picture taken?'"

A BOOK ABOUT CHICKENS

Another memorable project involved Zita and a brood of chickens. "When Zita was 5," Nellie said, "her plan was to get some chickens and sell the eggs, then get a goat and sell the milk, then finally get a horse. That was her life plan at the time."

"When she was 7," Nellie went on, "she had the opportunity to get the chickens and she was very excited about it. She talked about her chickens continuously and the rest of us got fed up with it. We told her, 'We don't want to hear any more about how this or that chicken was pecking at the corn because they all do the same thing: they peck at the corn.' And we added, 'Why don't you just write a book about it?' And she said, 'Well, maybe I will!'"

"That's how it all started, but that wasn't the language component of it. The language component came into place because the only person that we know fairly well who knows anything about chickens is my aunt in Hungary, who's 80 years old and has had chickens all her life. I grew up in the city and I knew nothing about chickens. So whenever Zita had a question about chickens—chickens with skin issues, molting chickens, egg-laying—she would ask my mom when we were on Skype, and my mom would ask my aunt, then my mom would tell us what my aunt said. And all of this was in Hungarian. So from the very beginning, it was obvious that my aunt would have to read this book, because she contributed so much to it, but she would have to read the Hungarian version."

With Nellie's help, Zita wrote the book in English, which was published as *Dixie's Chicken Sisters*, when she was 9. Nellie then took on the task of translating the 90-page book into Hungarian, and discussed the translated text with Zita along the way.

Finally, they published the Hungarian edition, too, and by this time word had spread among family and friends in Hungary who were eager to read Zita's book. During their next trip to Hungary, they brought along 50 copies, which were all handed out prior to their return home.

While this book project generated productive engagement in the minority language, Nellie emphasized that, like the project with Alfonzo, it created a positive impact on Zita's life, and the lives of others, in additional ways, too. "One of the biggest things, I think, is the fact that both of these projects are out of the ordinary," she said. "When I think back on my childhood, I don't necessarily remember getting up every morning and going to school, but anything that was out of the ordinary—for example, 'Remember that time we got stuck in the car on that one trip?'—those are the things that we remember. So, with these two projects, I guess I tried to create some experiences that are going to be memorable for them."

A year of immersion in Hungary

Nellie is now also scheming to create another memorable experience in her children's lives, one that can have an even more powerful impact on their language ability and cultural understanding. Despite the substantial progress in Hungarian that Zita and Zalán have made, Nellie recognizes that their lifestyle in the U.S. inherently limits the children's exposure and need for this language. In order to fuel a bigger breakthrough in the development of their Hungarian side, she plans to spend a year in Hungary with them while they're still young to immerse them in the language and culture. If possible, Scott will join Nellie and the kids for at least part of this time.

Nellie feels that it's important to pursue this plan in the near future, not only for the significant impact it can have on Zita and Zalán while they're still young, but also because they may grow less willing to take part at an older age. "I remember being an exchange student when I was 16," she explained, "and I wouldn't have wanted to do an exchange year with my family because I was already a teenager and I didn't want to be chaperoned by my parents in a different country." At the same time, she also wonders whether they would choose to spend time there by themselves when they're older. "Out of all the places they could go to, why would they be foreign exchange students in Hungary?"

She continued, "So there's a time push on this: If I want to be part of it, I have to do it before they become teenagers. And this way, we can all share the experience of being there together."

AFTERWORD: In fact, during the period of time in which I wrote this book, Nellie was able to move forward with her dream of realizing an immersion year abroad. She and the kids are now living in Hungary and Zita and Zalán are attending school there. As she told me, "For the first time in their lives, they live in the city, not in the country, and they're exposed to Hungarian all day, every day. They have to converse, do their schoolwork, and play in Hungarian. They also take tests and have oral exams almost daily, things that they never had to do while being homeschooled. For the first time, they're receiving continuous exposure to the minority language, paired with an inescapable need." While Nellie and her children had communicated mainly in English while in the U.S., they have evolved into using mostly Hungarian now. And when they speak with Scott, back at home in the U.S., they switch smoothly to English. Nellie acknowledged that it took several months for the kids to get used to communicating mainly in Hungarian, but that this transition caused no real concerns and, in fact, that they have all experienced this process as "humorous rather than frustrating." She explained, "For many weeks, Zalán would insert Hungarian words in his conversations with his dad. Or occasionally, they take English verbs and conjugate them in Hungarian, or use a Hungarian word and add 'ing' at the end, like the English verb form 'reading' or 'writing.' But as we spend more time here, these mistakes are gradually disappearing." As Nellie emphasized, this has been a natural shift in language use for the children, with rapid and continuing growth in their bilingual ability, and she expects the remainder of their time in Hungary to bring even more rewarding progress in their language development and cultural understanding.

CONTACT & RESOURCES FOR NELLIE

✉ korneliakr@gmail.com

🌐 proz.com/profile/744559

📖 *Dixie's Chicken Sisters* (her daughter's book)

19

Perseverance Amid the Dominance of the Majority Language

- Ana Paula was born in Brazil, but moved to the U.S. when she was a child. She speaks Portuguese, English, and Spanish, and works as a trilingual speech-language pathologist and clinical professor. She maintains a helpful website for speech-language pathologists, educators, and parents called The Speech Stop (thespeechstop.com) and is the author of the e-book *Practical Bilingualism* and a leveled set of storybooks for children, in English and Spanish, titled *Grow! Language Development with Engaging Children's Stories.*

- Her husband, Shawn, is American. He speaks English and has some passive ability in Portuguese. He works as a field inspector for commercial lenders.

- They have two children: a daughter, Rebekah, 11 years old, and a son, Caleb, 9.4 years old.

- The family lives in the U.S. state of Kansas.

Ana Paula was a bilingual child herself. She was born in Brazil, but moved to the U.S. when she was almost 11, saying that her father had been "infatuated" with the idea of living in this country. But before the whole family could immigrate—including Ana Paula, there were 10 children—her older siblings came to the U.S. first as exchange students. After attending college and getting married, they were then able to help the rest of the family join them.

When Ana Paula arrived in the U.S., she spoke only Portuguese. Because her parents were still tying up the loose ends of their life in Brazil, she lived with an elder brother and his American wife for several months and began attending a local elementary school. Apart from speaking Portuguese with her brother and the other younger siblings, she was "fully immersed" in English and this immersion helped fuel her quick progress.

Still, her lack of English ability was sometimes a source of stress during that early period of acquisition. She recalled struggling with homework assignments and scratching her head over the meaning of idiomatic expressions. And then there was a "traumatic moment" in P.E. class. "For whatever reason," she said, "we were learning how to shoot a BB gun and I didn't understand the directions and I ended up firing at somebody. I didn't hurt them, but I remember the P.E. teacher was screaming at me and I was crying."

Yet despite these difficulties, by the time her parents joined them for good in the U.S., "we were much more comfortable speaking English," she said.

Mother maintains Portuguese at home

While Ana Paula often had to use English while staying with her elder brother—because he worked full-time and his wife spoke no Portuguese—once she was reunited with her parents, they prohibited the younger children from using English at home. "My mom was ahead of her time," she explained. "She understood that if she didn't continue speaking to us in Portuguese, that essentially we would become strangers. Because it took them a good seven, eight years to really become comfortable in English. And so she would forbid us from speaking English with them. She couldn't control what we did with each other so among ourselves—like my brother and sister closest in age to me—we would speak English a lot of the time. But with my parents, it was always Portuguese."

Thus, because of her mother's persistence, Portuguese continued to be the family's main means of communication, even after they resettled in the U.S. and the children embarked on new lives in English. At the same time, Ana Paula's own growing interest in language development enabled her to advance her Portuguese in ways that her siblings did not.

"Spanish was my undergraduate major," she said, "and I did a ton of linguistics classes. I thought I was going to be a linguist, but when I found the field of speech-language pathology, the therapeutic component of working with people was very appealing to me. That seemed like a better fit for me than linguistics, but I took it upon myself to continue reading and writing in Portuguese and I just did a lot more than my siblings did to maintain it."

She went on, "When I studied Spanish, I also had to read and write in Spanish. So keeping up with that also helped me keep up with Portuguese. And then I became like the official interpreter of the family. So if anybody needed anything translated or interpreted in any language, whether it was Portuguese, Spanish, or English, I was their point person. And this just thrust me into the position of constantly using these languages."

As a result, while her siblings were able to remain fluent speakers of Portuguese, their literacy level in this language is less developed. And, over the years, Portuguese has not been the same high priority in their lives as it has been for Ana Paula. "None of them have spoken Portuguese at home to their own kids," she said. "Out of 10 children, I was the only one who felt that that was important. My parents instilled the same thing in all of us, but, for whatever reason, I'm the only one who clung to it."

Creating connections through Portuguese

From the beginning of her bilingual journey with her kids, Ana Paula's motivation has been tied to the idea of creating connections, both with her Brazilian family and with her own Brazilian identity.

She explained, "I didn't want there to be a barrier between my kids and my parents, or my kids and their aunts and uncles and cousins in Brazil because, to me, it was so important that they connect in a very tangible way with my kids. I didn't want there to be a language barrier to somehow impede that connection. Even though my parents speak English, their heart language will always be Portuguese. And even though they can converse at a superficial level with their other grandkids, it's very different with my own kids because they were able to connect with them in a different way. So that, to me, was huge and made it all worthwhile in terms of the labor that's involved in trying to pull this off, especially in a country where bilingualism isn't valued and there are very limited resources for Portuguese."

She then described the importance of her bilingual aim in regard to her children's connection to her and to their heritage. "I didn't feel that my kids could really know me fully if they didn't know Portuguese. It's a part of who I am. And not just the language, but my culture and my Brazilian-ness, and I can't really pass that down to them outside of them speaking Portuguese. So I wanted them to feel that same connection, though I know they'll experience it differently than I did because they're not fully Brazilian. However, I feel like I've been able to give them enough of our language and our culture so they do feel part Brazilian even though, technically, they're not by birth."

Clearly, Ana Paula's personal motives for wanting to hand down her Portuguese ability to her children are deeply felt and have driven her daily efforts over the years. At the same time, she credits the fact that her husband has always empathized with her bilingual aim for their kids. "He saw the value of what I was doing," she said. "He supported me 100%, to the point where he had to subject himself to being lost, a lot of the time, in our home because I was speaking to the kids in Portuguese and I would translate as much as I could for him, but there are still gaps, you can't do a hundred percent translation of everything. So he subjected himself to being the outsider for a while. Now he understands quite a bit; he can't speak it, but he understands a lot. If I had a different kind of husband, it would have been hard to maintain this, to be as passionate and as dedicated as I was, especially early on."

Experiencing a shift when schooling began

When Ana Paula became pregnant with her daughter, at the age of 30, she had already been living in the U.S. for 20 years. "In terms of baby language, kids' songs, children's stories, poems, finger plays, I felt very rusty as far as that went in Portuguese. I felt like I needed to make Portuguese feel natural with my kids and so I made a conscious effort to relearn all those things. So my first step, while I was pregnant, was immersing myself in baby stuff."

With the aim of using Portuguese more confidently with her first child, she bought up all the Portuguese baby books and CDs she could find. These resources then enabled her to expand her knowledge of the words and expressions that Portuguese speakers use with babies and small children, while also adding to her repertoire of children's songs, which she learned by writing down the lyrics and memorizing them.

During the first five or six years, Ana Paula said she was "fairly methodical and consistent" about speaking Portuguese to her kids and providing them with language exposure through books, music, video, and other resources. She also homeschooled them for a few years—until her daughter was in second grade and her son was in first grade—so she could maintain as much input in Portuguese as possible while also nurturing their literacy in this language.

The first phase of their bilingual journey, then, when Ana Paula was able to spend substantial time with the children and provide them with ample exposure in Portuguese to effectively counter the English input from their father and from the wider community, was marked by rewarding progress. Rebekah and Caleb, she said, were using Portuguese quite actively each day.

Once the children started school, however, the family entered a new phase and the balance of exposure between Portuguese and English became heavily weighted toward English. Along with the continuing English exposure at home, there was now English exposure from the school day, from homework, and from friends. Under these circumstances, Ana Paula, who is essentially the sole source of the minority language, has found it far more challenging to advance their Portuguese and maintain its active use, describing herself as "a minority language gnome battling the majority language giant." At this point, she said, the kids are still quite capable of communicating in Portuguese, but their English has grown more dominant and thus they use Portuguese less actively than they did before.

"I still do as much as I'm able," she said, referring to her daily efforts to support their Portuguese side, "but I always feel like it's not enough. And the other factor that has changed in our lives is when they started going to school, I started working full-time. Before, I was either not working or I was working part-time so I don't get to do some of the things that I used to do. For example, we're reading less at home. I've tried to do more audio books in the car, but it's not the same as when I'm sitting down with them and reading a book."

The dominance of the majority language

Like many bilingual families in the world, Ana Paula's family experienced a dramatic shift in circumstances when the children began attending school in the majority language. And these circumstances have created challenging shortcomings in the two "core conditions" of exposure and need, thus impacting the development and use of the minority language. Along with the significant tilt toward more input in English and less input in Portuguese, she also pointed to the fact that her children don't generally feel a strong need to speak Portuguese, considering that everyone in their day-to-day lives—including their mother—is fluent in English.

"Whether it's church, school, extracurricular activities, piano, sports, everything is in English," she said. "So they don't feel that inherent need to speak. I'm constantly speaking to them in Portuguese, but they're responding in English. Sometimes they'll say something in Portuguese, but their default is almost always English. When we go to Brazil, all of a sudden, they start speaking Portuguese a lot more. And I'm like, 'Why don't you do this when we're at home?' And they say, 'Because at home, we don't feel like we need to.' So the need component comes into play where the need is inherently not there in any facet of their lives because every single environment they're in, there are English speakers."

While pleased with the fact that her children have developed competence in Portuguese and are capable of using it when they feel a stronger need to do so, Ana Paula acknowledged that their reluctance to speak this language more actively at home, as they once did, has been a source of frustration. "It makes me feel like I'm doing something wrong," she said. "There's that guilt of, what can I do to change this? But honestly, I feel the need component is against me. I can provide all the exposure I want, but my exposure won't trump need."

Still, Ana Paula has experienced enough success on her journey to date to know that her perseverance will continue to pay off. So, despite the difficulties of this stage, she persists in trying new tactics at home to encourage her children's use of Portuguese. "I'll say to them, 'If you're going to ask me a question, or ask me for something, it has to be in Portuguese, okay?' And it's funny because my son will come up to me and he'll ask me something in English and I'll feign ignorance or stupidity then he'll immediately switch and he'll ask it in Portuguese." She went on, with a laugh, "One time I said to them, 'Whatever you ask me, if it's in Portuguese, the answer is yes!'"

Earning the rewards of perseverance

A parent's ability to persevere over the long term, in the face of struggles and discouragement, ultimately depends on having an "anchor," she said. "If the odds are against you, as in my situation, you have to first determine what your motivation is. Why do you want to do this? Sometimes parents who want their kids to be bilingual, it's more like, 'Oh, I just think it would be cool.' Yeah, it's cool to be bilingual. Sure it is. But being cool is not going to get you through this. I think you have to have a deeply-rooted desire, reason, rationale, something that really keeps pushing you forward because the easy route is monolingualism. So when you're discouraged, when it doesn't seem like it's working, or when you feel like your attempts aren't producing what you want them to produce, then you go back to what drives you. For me, I'm trying to do this gigantic task and I feel all this pressure and lack of opportunity and resources. I feel these deficits in the midst of it all. But when I go back to my goal and the reason that I'm doing this, it's easy for me to just keep plowing ahead, you know?"

She continued, "And when we're in Brazil, I see the fruit. When I see my kids being able to quickly integrate with their cousins, when I see my aunts being able to affectionately have this interaction with them and they can reciprocate that, to me, that's the payoff. And that's worth more than anything—I can't even put a value on it."

Ana Paula then shared a story, a defining moment for her, which conveys the nature of the bilingual journey for many parents: that despite the difficulties and frustrations we encounter, when we nevertheless persist from day to day, from year to year, our efforts will inexorably generate gratifying progress over time. Beyond the obstacles, there is the reward of enabling our children to gain a deep grounding in the target language, a foundation that comes to feel like an organic part of who they are and will surely remain integral to their identity for the rest of their lives.

"I went on a work trip," she said. "I was presenting at a conference and I was gone for three or four days. For a couple of days I wasn't able to talk to the kids because by the time I was done, they were already in bed. When I finally talked to my daughter, I spoke to her in Portuguese, like I always do. I said, 'Hi Rebekah! How was your day?' And she said, 'Oh Mommy, I missed hearing your voice.' And I said, 'Oh really?' But then she said, 'I missed hearing Portuguese.' It wasn't so much my voice, it was me interacting with her in Portuguese, that bond, that connection. It was so sweet, one of those, 'Okay, I needed that.' It was kind of like my tank was getting empty and I needed that to recharge me."

AFTERWORD: When the bilingual aim is made a high priority in our lives, and when we sustain enough perseverance to press on with our best efforts from day to day, considerable success is bound to follow over the years of childhood. And this is true no matter what our conditions and difficulties may be. Though the basic circumstances of Ana Paula's journey have presented large challenges to her bilingual aim—and it's understandable why she views herself as a "minority language gnome" battling the "majority language giant"—it's nevertheless a story of *prevailing past obstacles*, rather than being thwarted by them, in order to fuel ongoing progress and fulfill the original goal of bilingualism for her children. This combination of priority and perseverance also explains how Ana Paula's story of bilingualism has differed significantly from the stories of her siblings. In order for languages and cultures to be handed down successfully to the next generation, parents must make this aim a central force in the family's lifestyle. This means persisting with the sort of enduring efforts pursued by the parents in this book, which also includes making the most of any support that might be available from other minority language speakers and settings. And by pressing on like Ana Paula, even when your tank is running low, you will inevitably bring about the same kinds of rewarding, recharging moments on your own bilingual journey.

CONTACT & RESOURCES FOR ANA PAULA

- ⊕ thespeechstop.com (professional site)
- ⊕ sperostuttering.org (nonprofit site)
- [f] facebook.com/anapaula.mumy.3979489
- [f] facebook.com/sperostuttering
- 📖 *Practical Bilingualism: A Concise and Simple Guide for Parents Raising Bilingual Children* (available at thespeechstop.com)
- 📖 *GROW! Language Development With Engaging Children's Stories* (available at northernspeech.com)
- ▶ TEDx talk "Placing Value on Human Imperfection" (youtu.be/pUVtGnGmHE8)

20

Bilingual Success and Children with Developmental Differences

▸ Eugene is originally from England and has lived in Japan for 25 years. A university English professor, he is also involved in research concerning bilingualism and children with Autism Spectrum Disorder (ASD) and other developmental issues. He maintains a Facebook group called Bilingual Children with Developmental Differences.

▸ His wife, Hanako, is Japanese and they are each proficient in the other's language.

▸ They have two children: a son, Teeda, 12.5 years old, and a daughter, Ursula, 10.6 years old.

▸ The family lives on the outskirts of a large Japanese city.

In many ways, the bilingual journey pursued by Eugene and his family is very similar to other families. What makes their journey different from most, however, is the special challenge that emerged when their son, their first child, was still small.

Eugene was born and raised in an Irish family in London. After graduating from university in England, his introduction to Japan "was a completely random thing," he said, explaining that a teaching job materialized and he took it. After three years in Japan, he returned to London and met Hanako there.

"It's significant, I think, that we met in England and that our language of communication was English from the get-go. That's remained the case, and compared to other families, that's been a crucial thing to help our kids keep the language going."

Eugene and Hanako moved back to Japan before they had children. When I asked if they had discussed their bilingual aim in advance, Eugene told me, "When Teeda was on the way, we talked about it and we agreed that we would speak only English at home—to each other, and also to our son. Outside of our home, we would use whichever language was appropriate."

Thus, from the very start, Teeda, and then Ursula, received strong exposure to the minority language from both parents. And yet, when Teeda turned 4, the family abruptly came to a crossroads in their continuing use of English.

Diagnosis drives new direction

Eugene explained that some questions had been raised about Teeda's development during early assessments of his growth. "They were slightly concerned about things like his reaction time and eye contact," he said. "But his general behavior wasn't what I would have imagined for someone who was autistic. He was very tactile, very warm and not afraid of people, and didn't have any sensory issues. He just seemed normal, for want of a better word. We knew that he was a bit quiet, that his expressions were a bit limited, but we thought it was within the possibility of just bilingual delay."

Compounding the situation was a year in which Eugene had to live apart from the rest of the family because he and Hanako were holding down jobs in two different cities. This period proved to be very upsetting for Teeda. Eugene said, "We thought that maybe this disruption was also a part of what was going on with him, that he was traumatized by that."

Then, after another regular assessment, and further testing beyond that, they received the news: their little boy was diagnosed with a mild form of ASD. "By the time it came, it wasn't like a shock. We had started to think that there was something going on with him. It wasn't beyond what we'd considered or discussed...but actually, to take that back, it *was* a shock. It was a real blow. It was just a very intense moment."

He continued, "At that point, the thing that sticks in my mind was the question of whether or not to keep the English going.

Instinctively, I worried that if he was struggling with language altogether, that trying to keep both English and Japanese would place an unreasonable burden on him. This apparently common sense position has tended until recently to be supported by doctors and teachers, not just in Japan but around the world. I felt panicked because I was really afraid of losing that direct connection with my kid. But if that was just about me being selfish, and if it's not what he needed, then I shouldn't do that. So I was questioning myself and, at the same time, I was questioning what we should do. The only logical path I could see was to try and find out more, learn more about the whole thing. And that's what started my research."

Decision guided by science

At the same time, Eugene said, Hanako was concerned about the idea of maintaining both languages. While she didn't insist that English be dropped, she wanted some reassurance that continuing their bilingual aim would be in their son's interest. And so Eugene's efforts to research this question became the basis for reaching a decision at this key juncture of their journey. In fact, it was a decision that would be a defining moment for their family's future, one way or another.

"Yeah, it was a huge moment," he said, "and that moment is the core shareable thing that I've gone through, feeling a full-on fight or flight response, like, 'I must do this. I must do that. I must try harder. I must be a perfect parent.' Then not knowing in which direction to turn your energy and also feeling alone, which isn't true, in a sense, once you reach out. But in the moment you don't know. And the evolution from that state of darkness and panic was on two fronts: increasing my knowledge—looking at the papers relevant to this dilemma—and then, equally important, connecting with other parents in a similar situation."

Eugene was also able to connect with a research group that was exploring this very topic—bilingualism in children with developmental differences—and they invited him to join their efforts to shed greater light on the science behind this question. Though the topic was quite new at the time, and the research already available was limited, he said that he couldn't find "a single paper" which suggested that children with a developmental difference who were capable of acquiring one language would not be capable of acquiring multiple languages. "Essentially, you can have levels of autism where any kind of language is not a realistic goal. But if you have a child with a developmental difference—and they've looked at many different conditions, including autism—and the child can handle one language, then being bilingual doesn't impede their development in any meaningful way."

Eugene said that subsequent studies carried out over the years, involving a range of languages and locations in the world, have continuously confirmed this finding. And not only is bilingualism not harmful to the linguistic and cognitive development of autistic children, "There's also a growing body of evidence that the meta-cognitive abilities that come with bilingualism can be very helpful for kids on the spectrum who struggle with executive function, and this can, in fact, enable them to perform better at certain tasks than if they were monolingual."

He added that, conversely, there are case studies of children with autism who were forced to be monolingual in the majority language based on the notion that children with developmental delays can only learn one language at a time. And as a consequence, they often became detached from family members who were minority language speakers and not as proficient in the majority language. Thus, dropping the minority language not only negates the various advantages that bilingualism can bring, it may create distinct disadvantages for the child and the family. With regard to Teeda, Eugene said, that would have meant "cutting him off from half of his family and his identity."

Moving forward, with support

In this deliberate way, Eugene and Hanako were able to gain the confidence to continue their bilingual journey as a family. "The first six months or so," he said, "was the darkest period and then it began to move towards more understanding and more peace, at least regarding that question. Particularly when I met the research group and started to talk to them, and talk with other researchers in the field, I got massive reassurance from that. We thought, all right, bilingualism should be okay. We were a bit nervous about it, but having made a decision, everything that came from then on just affirmed what we thought was right. But our general struggle with helping him through his condition, and helping ourselves through his condition, was a longer story."

While English continued to serve as the family's main language, they began providing more active support for Teeda's Japanese side, too. At the same time, Teeda was receiving support for his developmental needs through regular sessions of speech-language therapy and physical therapy. Though most of this therapy was in Japanese, they were also able to access some therapy in English.

"He continued all that through kindergarten," Eugene said, "and then, gradually, he kind of came out of his shell and developed, so the need for it seemed less. Today the main issue is concentration. His head is a very lively and busy place and so, in a classroom environment, concentrating is hard for him. That's his main academic issue."

"He's not as fluent in either language as our daughter is," he explained, "but it's not a question of language therapy, really. The kind of therapy he gets now, one evening a week, is for kids with developmental issues. They're helping him with how to approach his homework and writing and coping with these kinds of things."

Naturally, Teeda is a standout in his English classes at school, but he has more difficulty keeping up with the other subjects because, Eugene said, "his mind is so busy." In primary school, while officially belonging to the special needs class, he was encouraged to try as many mainstream classes as he could manage. In this way he was gradually able to take part in all mainstream classes, except Japanese, an achievement for which he felt proud. "In spite of this," Eugene continued, "we agreed with our son that he would start junior high still based in the special needs class. This is because it allows him to go on trying as many mainstreams classes as he's capable of, while still maintaining support for his weaker subjects. If he joined as a regular member of the mainstream program, this support would no longer be accessible."

Efforts benefiting both kids

While Eugene's family has had to address challenges that go beyond what most bilingual families must face, in other ways the bilingual success they're experiencing with both Teeda and Ursula is the result of the same kinds of efforts pursued by other families.

Since the very start of their journey, Eugene and Hanako have been generating ample exposure to the minority language within their home, especially through speech and through books. "I'm a great lover of books," Eugene said. "And I think that if you can get them to a point where they can pick up and enjoy books by them-selves, then it's an awesome engine for growth." He said that his kids can now read well in both languages, but acknowledged that getting them to read in the minority language is becoming harder. Like many families, as the children get older, they get busier with their lives in the majority language, which limits the time and energy they have for literacy activities in the minority language. He mentioned making use of manga and graphic novels in English in order to help motivate them to read.

In addition to these daily efforts embedded within their lifestyle in Japan, they have prioritized an annual trip to England, where the kids can spend about three weeks immersed in the language and culture. "Thanks to that, they have a strong connection with their family in England. They've got cousins their own age and my aunts and uncles have a strong bond with them, so that's been an important part of their language development. It's like a living thing where they have family and friends and it's all about English."

Eugene added that the Irish love of lively storytelling—in the form of his father's humorous tall tales—has also had a positive impact on his children. Referring to Ursula, Eugene said that these experiences have sparked her own creative spirit, motivating her to write stories and make picture books in English.

Lending support to other families

Eugene's experience as a parent and researcher of bilingual chil-dren with developmental differences has led him to become an active source of support for other families who are facing this same challenge. The Facebook group he initiated, Bilingual Children with Developmental Differences, now has hundreds of members around the world and serves as a community where advice and encouragement are freely shared.

I asked Eugene to offer his best advice for parents who have a child that has been diagnosed with ASD or another developmental issue. He responded by first underscoring the central point he made earlier, saying, "The scientific consensus is that if the child is capable of one language, then there is no detriment to them learning other languages, regardless of whatever issues they have. So, I would encourage them not to feel intimidated into giving up bilingualism for their child if their instincts tell them it may be beneficial."

At the same time, Eugene recommends that parents look at the research themselves to make the most informed decisions they can. "Through my experience, I learned how important it is to understand the science," he said.

He also stressed, "It really helps to reach out to others. I encourage parents to talk about it, to find people who understand their situation. Connect with others to share the load, to share experiences and ideas. Having this kind of connection was a great source of strength for us. The best kind of ally in this situation is someone who has already been there."

Reflecting on the distance his family has traveled together on their journey, Eugene noted, "Now, I have to kind of remind myself that my son is on the ASD spectrum. To me, he's just Teeda. When I talk to other parents who are in the situation I was in then, and how frantic they are in thinking how everything is going wrong and it's all just too much, I want to help them see that once you get through the panic phase, you start to understand that your child is just a kid, like any other kid, and more than you imagine, things will actually be okay."

AFTERWORD: As Eugene has stressed, children with developmental differences generally have the potential to become bilingual, too, if the same core conditions of exposure and need are adequately met. If the child is capable of learning one language, he or she is capable of learning more than one language, and there can be keen advantages for the child and family in continuing to nurture this process of bilingual development, in pressing on with their larger bilingual journey. At the same time that Eugene's story is an encouraging example for families with children who have developmental differences, his actions over the years, in addressing this challenge within his own family, are also an inspiration in another way. In fact, they demonstrate the idea that not only can our efforts to overcome life's difficulties benefit our own lives for the better, such efforts, when shared with the world, can benefit the lives of others who face a similar challenge. Clearly, that has been the case with Eugene in so generously sharing his experience as a parent, his knowledge as a researcher, and his advice as a leader of this growing worldwide community of bilingual families that include children who have ASD and other developmental differences.

CONTACT & RESOURCES FOR EUGENE

✉ eugeryan@gmail.com

𝗳 Facebook Group – Bilingual Children with Developmental Differences: facebook.com/groups/155717381272532

📖 Ryan, E. (2020, May 4). Sharing a Diagnosis of Autism for your Child. Oasis: Bulletin of the Connections Forum, 1(1). Retrieved 2020, June 11, from www.multiculturaljapan.com/oasis-bulletin-volume-1-issue-1.html

📖 Ryan, E. (2020) Navigating Public Education in Japan for a Third-Culture Child with Autism. In Cook, M.L., & Kittaka, L.G. (Eds.), Intercultural Families and Schooling in Japan: Experience, Issues, and Challenges (pp. 205~226). Candlin & Mynard ePublishing, Ltd.

🌐 eugespoems.wordpress.com

The Teenage Years and Beyond

The third stage of the journey continues the challenge of providing exposure in the minority language as well as opportunities for the child to use it actively. Compared to the second stage, when their kids were in primary school, parents often find that the time they can spend together with their teenage children, and the influence they have on their children's lives, shrinks even more significantly. Still, ongoing efforts, to the extent possible, can continue to strengthen the child's proficiency, with regular reading in the minority language especially helpful for advancing literacy and overall language ability. Approaching independence, bilingual children will then be poised to take over the journey themselves into their adulthood.

21

When the Larger Arc of Success Is a Freely Bilingual Family

- ▶ Alisa is originally from the U.S. and has lived in France for over 20 years. She is fluent in English and French and works from home as a web developer.

- ▶ Her husband, Frédéric, is French. Along with his mother tongue, he is proficient in English. He works as a flight dispatcher for an airline.

- ▶ They have two sons: Benjamin, 13.9 years old, and Noah, 11.6 years old.

- ▶ The family lives in a small village about an hour north of Paris.

- ▶ They also have a dog named Gala who, Alisa reports, is a "passive bilingual" in French and English, capable of understanding speech in both languages.

In the midst of the busy days of a bilingual journey, it can be difficult to clearly see the larger arc of success that a family is on course to experience over the full length of the childhood years. After all, we can't exactly know what that longer outcome will be when we're still years away from arriving there.

In Alisa's family, both parents are proficient in the majority language and the minority language. And like other families out in the world where the parents have dual language proficiency, hers seems to be navigating the same sort of long-term evolution in their use of the two languages.

1. Early on, extra emphasis is placed on the minority language and such efforts provide this language with a head start.

2. When schooling begins, the balance tilts back toward the majority language, which then grows more dominant.

3. As the children grow older, and the parents continue their efforts to advance the minority language, the family eventually arrives at a stage where all members are capable enough, and comfortable enough, to use both languages freely within the family unit, according to their preferences and needs.

While Alisa may currently feel some concern over the development of her children's minority language side—with her sons now 13 and 11—the continuing efforts that she and her husband make can enable the family to ultimately fulfill their quest toward becoming a "bilingual family" in the fullest sense of that expression.

Early emphasis on English

Alisa paid her first visit to France as a sophomore in college, then returned the following year for a junior year abroad. After she graduated, she came back again, and with the addition of Frédéric in her life, decided to stay.

Before they had children, Alisa and Frédéric communicated in French, but then switched to English and adopted the ml@home approach during their sons' early years. She explained, "We started out speaking English all the time, with the idea that they would be going to school in France and getting plenty of French input once they started school."

Underlying this approach were their deeper motivations for pursing a bilingual aim. "One of the most important things for us, of course, was that they be able to communicate with their grandparents in the U.S. because I've seen some families where the grandchildren don't speak the same language as the grandparents and that just seems so sad. Beyond that, being able to speak English will open up opportunities for them in their careers, no matter what they do."

As it turns out, their early emphasis on English not only fueled their children's development in this language, it advanced Frédéric's ability in English as well. In fact, Alisa has also been mindful of supporting his own improvement over the years, telling me, "Sometimes I look for resources for my husband, too, like books and novels about airplanes."

French catches up quickly

During those first few years, Alisa and Frédéric stayed as consistent as they could about using English with each other and with their children. Alisa also credits the fact that she works from home, and could spend ample time with the kids, while Frédéric's schedule has enabled him to be very present in their lives as well.

At the same time, Alisa was quite proactive about bringing English books and other resources into their home and reading to them every day. She mentioned being a bookworm herself and was eager to read to her kids not only to help provide them with as much English input as possible but also because "I wanted to share my own childhood favorites with them."

Although most French children begin going to preschool the year they turn 3, Alisa and Frédéric chose to have Benjamin start a year later so he could have as much English input as possible before he became immersed in French. By that time, when Benjamin was 3 years and 9 months, Alisa said that his English had grown strong for his age but his French was "almost non-existent."

"When we first signed him up," she continued, "we talked to the preschool teacher and told him that Benjamin might not speak very much at the beginning. We just wanted to make sure the teacher knew so he didn't think that Benjamin was willfully ignoring him or not responding. But the teacher understood, and it wasn't a problem."

Asked if she had any concerns about Benjamin starting school without much ability in French, Alisa said, "No, it wasn't a worry for us at all because we knew that French would come once he was immersed in it at school."

At the same time that Alisa prepared the teacher for Benjamin's enrollment in the school, she also sought to prepare her son. "We made a point of telling him, 'You have to speak French at school. People won't understand you if you speak English. You have to speak French.'" She then added, with a laugh, "He definitely got the message, to the point where, when they had a class photo and the teacher told the kids to say 'cheese,' Benjamin said 'fromage'!"

As Alisa expected, Benjamin's language ability grew quickly and he was soon speaking French like the other children. "Of course, we're comparing 3-year-olds and their grammar and vocabulary isn't very advanced, anyway, so it didn't take long at all for him to catch up."

French becomes dominant

In fact, from that point, French evolved into Benjamin's more dominant language. Alisa recalled that he began speaking more French at home "because he was surrounded by it so much at school." This development, in turn, affected the language use between Benjamin and his younger brother, Noah: before Benjamin started school their default language was English; after that, it became, and now remains, French.

As both children continued their schooling, and French loomed larger in their daily lives, Alisa and Frédéric began using more French, too. In this way, the balance between the family's use of the two languages tipped gradually from English to French.

Alisa said, "That's one of the reasons we try to have people visit us as often as we can, people who speak only English, because it forces the kids to speak it. They know that Frédéric and I can speak both languages and so they go for the one that's easiest for them, and that's French."

Along with receiving regular English-speaking visitors, Alisa also continues to seek out English books and other resources that can strengthen their input and their interest. "Benjamin is a big reader," she said, "and since I try to buy only English books, he reads mainly in English and he likes reading in English. I often try to get him started on a series. I'll try out the first one in a series and if he gets into that one, he'll keep reading them, even multiple times."

Noah isn't yet as eager a reader as his older brother and Alisa is pleased if he reads in either language. When it comes to reading in English, "What's worked more for him are comic books, graphic novels, anything with lots of drawings."

Alisa also continues to read aloud to her sons as often as she can. If Frédéric is at work and unable to join them for dinner, she'll eat first, before the boys, then read to them during the meal. "That way they're a captive audience!" she said.

Trips to the U.S.

Another important part of their bilingual journey has been trips back to the U.S., at least once a year. Frédéric's job at the airline provides travel benefits that make such trips more affordable. Alisa said that these experiences of immersion not only enable the boys to engage in English and strengthen their language ability, they can also connect with their American side and stretch their cultural knowledge.

"I think it helps, too, with their attitude toward English," she said. "It makes them more positive toward it because they get to see that other people are using it, that it's useful somewhere. And, of course, when we go to the U.S., we're on vacation, there's no pressure, it's a happy time, so I think that also impacts their positive attitude toward it."

Studying English in school

When her sons were in elementary school, Alisa was able to arrange for them to spend the school's English lessons—the level of which was much lower than her sons' English level—doing more suitable English workbooks that she got from the U.S. However, when they entered middle school, she sensed that the teachers there wouldn't be as open to them doing separate work in the classroom. She acknowledged feeling some frustration over this situation, but has also come to see its positive aspects as well.

"I wouldn't say it's very useful, but I wouldn't say it's not useful, either," she said. "Of course, they're learning English as a foreign language, so it's not the same level that they would be learning in America or somewhere else. But it does give them an advantage. It gives them that one easy subject where they can stand out. And I guess in some ways it does help with grammar."

Speaking more English again

Over the years, Alisa has come to speak more French than English with her kids, but lately she is again making a greater effort to use English with them. "French has become the default, for everyone," she said. "I feel like, if that's too much the case, they're going to start losing their English ability, or they won't advance their English ability. So I've been making more of a conscious effort to speak to them in English."

While Benjamin has responded to her use of more English with more English of his own, Noah has been less receptive so far. "He will answer me in French if I speak to him in English," she explained. "And even if I try to encourage him to speak in English, he just won't, even though he can, perfectly well."

Alisa said she has seen this same dynamic in other families with an English-speaking partner. "The children understand English, but they won't speak it. And I don't want my kids to end up in that sort of situation, where they're not taking advantage of this big positive thing that they have."

Advancing their English ability

Alisa also pointed to the different personalities of her two sons—calling Benjamin more "reserved" and Noah more "outgoing"—and how she needs to keep this in mind as she works to nurture their English side. Benjamin, she said, is able to gain more exposure to English through books and reading, while Noah is more willing to engage in English through interaction, like when he befriended a boy from Thailand who had come to their community.

She stressed the importance of keeping the target language fun, too, sharing an example of how she made a creative change to the rules in a game of Scrabble so her kids would feel more motivated to play the game in English instead of in French. "I told them, 'You can play in French or in English, whatever you want, but when you play a word in English, you automatically get a triple word score.' And that worked really well!"

Through a variety of efforts—led by the desire to use English more proactively with her kids—Alisa hopes to continue fueling their progress through the teenage years, even to the point where they would be capable of studying at a university in the U.S. one day.

"As far as their speaking ability, I'm comfortable with where they are," she said. "The biggest thing I'm concerned about is their writing ability. If they were in America, they would be writing papers in English class and things like that and they're not doing that here. So I feel that, right now, that's a deficit. And I would like to see that improve."

With a number of years yet to go before the boys are grown, and a renewed emphasis on English within the family, progress will no doubt continue to be made toward this aim of stronger literacy—and that larger outcome of a freely bilingual family.

AFTERWORD: As the many stories in this book indicate, success at raising bilingual children can be realized in a range of ways. While this is also true of the goal of becoming a bilingual family, it should be pointed out that *timing* is often an important factor in this process. When a bilingual couple uses both languages freely, from the time the child is born, this may undercut both the amount of exposure given to the child in the minority language as well as the child's perceived need to actively use that language once he or she begins to speak. As Alisa's story shows, the early emphasis on English, their minority language, enabled the boys to develop a firm and active foundation in this language during those first few formative years. It may be true that French then grew more dominant, but they're still quite capable of using English when motivated to do so. The same is not always true when the majority language is given freer rein from birth. In such cases, the majority language may become too dominant too soon and prevent the child from developing sufficient competence and confidence in the minority language. Thus, the larger goal of becoming a bilingual family is then made more difficult because the timing of this freer use of the two languages occurred earlier in the process, when later might have proven more effective. While the goal of becoming a bilingual family is a wonderful and worthwhile aim, it behooves parents to consider how they can realize this aim most effectively. For many families, like Alisa's, this may mean first emphasizing the minority language, and even "de-emphasizing" the majority language, in order to fuel stronger progress in the child's bilingual development, and greater success as a fully bilingual family in the years ahead.

CONTACT FOR ALISA

✉ alisa.cognard@gmail.com

22

7 Languages in a Family of 5
(Plus a Secret Language in the Past)

▶ Ute grew up in Italy, raised by German parents. While her two native languages are German and Italian, she has also gained ability in a number of other languages. She works as a language consultant and intercultural communication trainer (utesinternationallounge.com).

▶ Her husband, Rolf, is originally from Switzerland. His native language is Swiss German, though he is also multilingual. He is a patent examiner at the European Patent Office.

▶ They live in the Netherlands with their three children: a son, Francesco, 16.8 years old, and twin daughters, Alice and Lucia, 13.3 years old.

▶ The family makes use of seven languages, to varying degrees, on a regular basis.

Ute has always led a multilingual lifestyle.

"My parents are German," she explained, "but when I was born, they were living in Italy. So I grew up in Italy and the community language was Italian. I spoke Italian with my friends."

At the same time, she attended a European school which had a German section. She started learning French at this school, from the age of 6, then English from the age of 11. She was also introduced to Latin at 13 and acquired some Dutch from friends at school. When she moved to Switzerland as a university student, she activated her passive ability in Swiss German, which she had previously developed through watching Swiss German TV programs. And she managed to pick up Spanish, too, from reading in this language and attending classes in literature and linguistics that were taught in Spanish.

While living in Switzerland, however, her ability in German began to falter because she was using mainly Italian and French in her work. "I was in my mid-20s," she recalled, "and I was almost unable to form a single sentence in German. I remember once I was on the phone with my mom, and I was switching back and forth between German and Italian because I know she understands Italian. She told me, 'Ute, finish the sentence in German.'" It was then that Ute realized she needed to return full circle and focus more on her mother tongue again.

A few years after Ute met Rolf, the couple moved to Italy, which is where their first child was born. When Francesco was still a toddler, the family moved to the Netherlands, which meant that Dutch was added to the mix of languages, too, bringing the total number to seven: German, Dutch, English, Swiss German, Italian, French, and Spanish.

Although nurturing seven languages is naturally a daunting challenge in some ways, Ute's own language learning experience has enabled her to hold a healthy perspective on this process with her children. She told me, "My goals are mainly that they enjoy the languages and that they want to improve them." While her efforts are focused most keenly on the three languages that the family has prioritized to date—namely, German, Dutch, and English—she stressed that the other languages can keep progressing over time, too, as long as the children are encouraged to continue engaging with them. Thus, the basic aim is *ongoing improvement*, not necessarily a certain language level. With this emphasis on the *process* of language development, rather than the *result*, growth itself equals success and gradually leads to ever higher levels of language ability.

Early changes and challenges

With seven languages—plus a "secret language" once spoken between the twins—the family's multilingual journey has been an ever-changing, ever-challenging adventure. This journey began, in fact, with Ute speaking Italian to Francesco, Rolf speaking Swiss German to him, and Ute and Rolf communicating in German (and sometimes in French or English, depending on who they were with). Explaining why she initially chose to speak Italian to her son, Ute said, "It's because I prefer Italian. It's my 'heart language,' my emotional language. We were living in Italy and I hoped that we would stay in Italy. But then we moved to the Netherlands when he was 2 and a half and he stopped talking to me in Italian. At first, I insisted and sometimes, yes, I managed to get him speaking Italian using different strategies. But we didn't have any peers for him to speak Italian with, which must have been a shock for him because he was used to playing with Italian-speaking children. All of a sudden everyone was talking in Dutch, so he preferred Swiss German, which sounds like Dutch in certain ways."

A year later, the twins were born and the first bits of language they eventually uttered were monosyllables in Italian, Swiss German, and Dutch. However, when the girls were 15 months old, they developed a "secret language" between the two of them. "It happened slowly," Ute said, "not from one day to the next. But I started not understanding what they were saying. I thought maybe they were just trying out sounds, but then I realized that they were talking to each other and saying things that maybe were similar, phonetically, to the other languages, but they lacked the meaning. Like one would say something and the other would just stand up, go in the kitchen, and take a spoon out of the drawer and come back. So they were understanding each other, but it was difficult for me to understand."

It was difficult for Francesco, too, Ute said, because he wanted to play with his sisters and felt very frustrated at not being able to communicate with them. After three months of this distress, Ute and Rolf, with Francesco in agreement, decided to switch to German for the whole family—the language that they had been using as a couple and the children had come to understand receptively—instead of pressing on with Ute's Italian and Rolf's Swiss German. "My son was very happy," she said, "and the girls stopped speaking the secret language within two weeks. Maybe they would have stopped anyway, or maybe it was because of the German. I don't know, but I didn't want to turn back to the other languages because I didn't want to trigger another phase of secret language."

Ute is unsure what prompted the twins to invent their own language, but wonders if it was a kind of "transition language" which enabled them to communicate with one another before they had developed enough fluency in any of the other languages to communicate. She added, "But it was a transition language that actually isolated them from the rest of the world, which was then, for me, a warning sign because, well, language is for communication. Yes, they could communicate with each other, but they were like an island. So it was very interesting, but also very worrying."

Juggling languages with a language plan

Though, at that point, German became the family's main language—along with Dutch from the community—Ute and Rolf didn't actually drop Italian and Swiss German. To a more limited degree, they continued to provide some input in these languages, too. So as the children grew there was still ongoing exposure to Italian and Swiss German through speech, books, and visits to locations where these languages are widely spoken. Ute stressed that this shift in language use—from German in the background to German in the foreground—was handled in a patient and thoughtful fashion. "We made sure the transition was smooth, increasing the use of German but keeping the other two languages very much alive in our daily routines. As all three children understood German, we didn't have to explain anything we said. I think this is very important as it made the transition more like a natural step for all of us."

"And when my son turned 11," she continued, "he came to me and said, 'Mom, I want to speak Italian with you.' So I said, 'Well, okay, let's see if the girls are okay with this, too.' But they weren't, so that's when we started making a language plan." Ute explained that this language plan, which is updated regularly, takes into account the needs and preferences of the children at any given time with regard to the family's multiple languages. So the focus of her efforts will continually shift from one language to another, child by child, in order to advance their progress in all of them to the degree possible.

"It's complex," she said, "and it changes over time. The children first went to a Dutch preschool, and then they began going to a British school, where they speak English. At that school, they also started studying Spanish and French. So I said, 'Okay, you now have Spanish and French at school. Do you want me to speak Spanish or French with you? Do you want us to read books in Spanish or French? Do you want us to watch videos in Spanish or French?'" In this way, Ute is able to make the most of her own multilingual ability as she seeks to cultivate the multilingual ability of her children.

"It's like juggling several balls and trying not to drop any," she said. "If they're struggling with one of the languages, or I see that they need a little more input, then I say, all right, we have to focus more on this." Ute mentioned that her daughter, Alice, needed special support for her language development throughout primary school for issues involving pronunciation and language mixing. These issues were making it hard for Alice to communicate clearly in English at school, but her teachers, without fully taking into account the multiple languages she was in the process of acquiring, assumed there was a learning problem. However, with the support of a speech therapist and Ute herself, Alice was able to gain greater mastery over her multilingual ability. Ute added, "Personally, I consider Alice's way of using languages to be fascinating on so many levels. She's a very talkative person and I think she expresses herself through this inventive language use."

The family's evolving language plan, then, serves as a tool for placing greater or lesser amounts of attention on each child's development in these languages, including newfound interest in additional languages, like Francesco's recent interest in learning Chinese. When I told Ute that "fluid" might be a good word to describe how she focuses and refocuses her efforts from child to child and language to language, depending on the needs of each new phase of their multilingual journey together, she laughed and said: "Or orderly chaos!"

Providing support to other families

Ute's personal experience leading a multilingual life, and success-fully raising multilingual children, has led to her professional work as a language consultant for other multilingual families. "I saw that there was a need for families who also juggle multiple languages to have some kind of system," she said. "So I help them make a family language plan, like the one I've made for my own family." In this way, she seeks to strengthen the multilingual success of other families by giving more structure to the parents' efforts so they can better meet the needs and preferences of their children.

Ute mentioned, too, that working with families can mean working with the parents in a kind of "couples therapy." She explained that it isn't uncommon for the majority language parent to lack the desire to learn the minority language, which leads the minority language parent to feel alone and frustrated without a "sparring partner." In order for the family's journey to proceed more enjoyably and effectively, she urges the majority language parent to "at least learn a little bit alongside the children. You don't have to become fluent. But if you can understand your children and your wife or husband, things will expand for the whole family."

Ute stressed that a family's experience of their bilingual or multilingual journey should be "healthy for everyone involved." This view reflects the sensible approach she has pursued with her own kids over the years, prioritizing the three most important languages while aiming for ongoing improvement in the other four. And for all seven languages, she has sought to align her efforts with their personal interests and emphasize their enjoyment of the family's multilingual adventures.

Like many parents on this path, the fact that there's no end to the actions that could potentially be taken makes Ute wonder if her efforts are "enough." But even if they aren't, she said, exhibiting the positive outlook that has defined her multilingual life, the children will be in a good position to continue learning these languages—and perhaps others, too—as they live out the years of their own multilingual lives.

AFTERWORD: As Ute conveys, through both her words and her actions, this journey to nurture multiple languages in our children—whether one more or many more—must be "healthy" for the whole family. The greater goal, then, as I emphasized at the beginning of this book, is not simply success at the bilingual or multilingual aim alone, but an overall experience of well-being and joy from day to day throughout this process. *Put plainly, what we want is not only a satisfying result, but a satisfying process, too.* Again, there are no perfect parents, and no perfect journeys from beginning to end, but when we continually seek both objectives—advancing our children's language development while also animating the experience itself with a healthy amount of well-being and joy—we can fulfill the most rewarding potential for our adventure as a family. Toward this end, I often encourage parents to be both *very serious* about their bilingual aim and yet *very playful* about how they pursue it. Balancing the two can be tricky, and it's a balance that must be mindfully managed on an ongoing basis, but the more serious we are about our aim, and the more playful we can be in our actions, the more success and joy we will very likely experience over the many years of this long quest.

CONTACT & RESOURCES FOR UTE

- ✉ info@UtesInternationalLounge.com
- 🌐 UtesInternationalLounge.com
- 𝐟 Facebook Group – Multilingual Families: facebook.com/groups/MultilingualFamilies
- 📷 @utesintlounge
- ▶ youtube.com/UtesInternationalLounge
- 📖 *The Toolbox for Multilingual Families* (co-authored with Ana Elisa Miranda)
- 📖 *How to raise a bilingual child. Practical guide for parents with ready to use activities* (co-author, available at www.bilingualfamily.eu/resources-for-parents/)
- ▶ Raising Multilinguals LIVE!, a bi-weekly broadcast on Facebook and YouTube with Rita Rosenback and Tetsu Yung

23

Engaging Children in the Minority Language with a Playful Spirit

- ▶ Amanda is originally from Taiwan and has lived in the U.S. for about 10 years in total. Since she and her husband had their two children, the family has experienced a series of relocations to a number of countries. Her mother tongue is Mandarin and she teaches Mandarin to children as Miss Panda Chinese (misspandachinese.com).

- ▶ Her husband, Ted, is American and works for the U.S. State Department. He has developed some passive understanding of Chinese.

- ▶ They currently live in Washington, D.C. and their two kids are Michael, 16.1 years old, and Emily, 14.3 years old.

- ▶ Along with English and Mandarin, the children have been exposed to Spanish, French, and Russian through their relocations.

Amanda is a prime example, I think, of a parent who has pursued the bilingual aim both very seriously and very playfully.

Her cheerful zest for language teaching and learning began when she was a small child in Taiwan. Her father had a passion for English and he handed down that passion to his daughter. "He was my first English teacher," she said. "English and other languages fascinated me even when I was young. Taiwan has so many dialects.

When I was growing up, my grandparents spoke a different dialect. And outside the house, I heard more people speaking different dialects, too. It was like a multilingual environment!"

Amanda started studying English formally in middle school when she was 13 years old. At the age of 15, she traveled to the U.S. with her mother to visit her aunt and cousins in San Francisco. "That was the first time I really used English," she said and shared a vivid memory of her aunt handing her 20 dollars and asking her to go get dinner for the family. Amanda found a Kentucky Fried Chicken and bravely used her still limited English to buy the food. "I came out with two bags full of chicken! And the dinner was fabulous! So I think that was a confidence booster and also showed me that language is for communication."

A few years later she then returned to the U.S. to study International Communications, minoring in Bilingual Education, at a university in Texas. It was there that she met Ted. After they got married, and were ready to have children, Amanda said they didn't think too much about the various strategies for raising bilingual kids. "Ted's native language is English and my native language is Mandarin so we thought that would be natural, we'd just do that."

Persevering past early challenges

Amanda said that, from the start, she spoke Chinese pretty consistently to her children. At the same time, with her son—her first child—she also felt some concern about speaking only Chinese. "I was a little bit worried," she recalled, "and you have people trying to influence you, saying things like, 'Oh, why are you doing this? He's not talking yet. See, everybody's talking, but he's not talking!' So you do have that kind of uncomfortable feeling. You're trying to figure out the right way, but you don't know because you've never walked this path before, so it takes a while. I think after the first year, or year and a half, I just said to myself, 'You know, everything's going to be okay. I'll only speak Chinese and it's going to be fine.' So, especially for the first child, I think there's some uncertainty."

Amanda's persistence paid off. Her children's ability in Chinese grew steadily, and they used it actively, alongside their ability in English. "But when my son was about 7 years old," she said, "he came to me one day—we were living in Hawaii at that time—and he told me, 'Mom, that's it. I'm not going to speak Chinese to you anymore. I'm only going to speak English.' So I said, 'Oh, really?' And he said, 'Yeah, Mom, you're the only person who speaks Chinese. Nobody else is speaking Chinese.'"

Amanda felt taken aback at that moment. "I was like, 'Oh no!' So I said, 'If you want to speak English, okay. But I'm only going to speak Chinese to you.'" She went on, "So I continued to speak Chinese and I did lots of fun things in Chinese with my daughter. And one day he saw us tossing marshmallows in different glasses, because we were doing Chinese characters, and he came up to me and said, 'I want to play. I want to speak Chinese. I'll speak Chinese to you.'"

This experience underscored for Amanda the importance of pursuing engaging ways to promote the minority language, drawing children toward it with fun, playful efforts. Still, she also realized that she had to do something more to respond to her son's feelings.

Expanding the influence of the minority language

"I decided 'home alone' is not a good thing. I needed to take this out of my home. That's why I decided to bring Mandarin to my daughter's preschool and to my son's elementary school." Although she met with some initial resistance from administrators, Amanda was able to convince them to give the idea a try: once a week, for 20 minutes, she would teach Chinese as a volunteer to each class of students at these two schools.

"It was phenomenal!" she said. "At the preschool, my daughter was my little teaching assistant and she totally loved it. And all the kids in her preschool class, they loved it, too. Even the parents told me, 'This is so much fun! Our kids are teaching us Mandarin!'"

At the elementary school, she experienced the same rewarding success, including with her son. "It was so cute," she said. "All the kids treated me like a star. When they spotted me on campus, even just picking up my kids, they would run up to me, yelling, 'Hi, Miss Panda!' And they would sing a Chinese song for me, or say something in Chinese—whatever I had taught them. At one point, my son pulled on my shirt when he saw some other kids running toward me. He said, 'Mom, tell them I'm your son and I speak Chinese, too.'"

"For my kids," she said, "Chinese was no longer just a home language. It was also a popular language at school."

Emphasizing a fun, playful approach

Amanda's work in the schools then inspired her to share her teaching ideas and materials with an even broader audience of families and schools by founding the Miss Panda Chinese website. She explained how some parents at the preschool had approached her about creating an audio CD so the opportunity for their children to learn Chinese at school could be extended at home as well. In addition to this CD, titled *Let's Learn Mandarin Chinese*, she has a new book, *First Mandarin Sounds: An Awesome Chinese Word Book*, that she hopes will be another engaging resource for children to learn this language.

In her efforts to nurture Mandarin in her children, as well as many more kids, Amanda has sought to engage them through a playful approach. "Being playful is so important because that's how I was able to keep going," she said, referring back to the uncertainty of the earlier years of her journey. "That's how my kids could say, 'Okay, I'll follow you. I want to see where you're taking me.'"

"And playfulness is not only for little kids," she added, emphasizing this point for older children and parents, too. "If you want to go far on this journey, there should be playfulness and fun along the way. That's why I say, 'If you're not having fun, your kids aren't having fun.'"

Nurturing literacy in Chinese, too

Amanda has also followed this principle in her efforts to nurture her children's literacy in Chinese. While books and reading have formed the foundation for these efforts, she also mentioned writing her own silly stories, making use of jokes and riddles, and playing board games which involve some reading. While she wants to engage them in literacy activities on a regular basis, she also recognizes the difficulty of reading and writing in Chinese and understands that her children's time and energy for this is limited. "If I challenge them too much," she said, "this could kill their interest. The content has to be fun. I want them to love the language. I don't want them to resent it."

Toward this end, she tries to stay disciplined and work with her kids each day for a short time, "at least 20 minutes," where they do some reading and a little writing. And by making this part of their lifestyle, she has managed to advance, in small increments, both their literacy development and their overall proficiency in Chinese.

"That's why parents need to be strong," she said. "A lot of my friends haven't been able to sustain this. They say, 'Let's just use English, it's so much easier.' I understand that. So I think we have to lead ourselves before we can lead our kids."

She also described how her efforts to nurture literacy and language proficiency are also tied to fostering cultural awareness. "I think culture is something so important and also so fascinating," she said. When they read traditional Chinese stories, or watch Chinese dramas or documentaries, such opportunities can stretch both language ability and background knowledge at the same time.

Trip to Taiwan highlights their success

Although Taiwan is a long and costly trip from the U.S., the family tries to go there every two years or so to see extended family. Meanwhile, they also make use of Skype and other digital ways to bridge this distance.

On their most recent trip to Taiwan, it became very clear to Amanda how far she and her kids have traveled on their bilingual journey together. "My son was able to do an interview with my 90-year-old father and listen to him talk about his life, all in Mandarin. That was so precious for me. Ten years ago, I couldn't even have imagined that happening. I was like, 'Wow, these kids, they've really tried hard.'"

At the same time, Amanda credits her husband for his continuous support over the years. Although he doesn't speak much Mandarin, he's been "learning along the way," she said, and can now understand quite a lot. "My husband has been a big part of this," she said. "He works with me and helps me keep going. Together is better, that's what I say. We have to work together."

Maintaining a positive, proactive outlook

While playfulness has been a central part of her approach, Amanda admitted with a laugh, "I'm not so fun all the time! I've told you all the fun stuff, but sometimes it was really hard. Over the years, when my kids were growing up, I didn't really have any Chinese family around me or a lot of Chinese friends. So I created my own community by going to the schools. They didn't need to be Chinese, you see. You can pass on whatever language you have to other people and create a different kind of community."

She continued, "I think the minority language is something you should be proud of. For the past 12 years, I've been doing a Lunar New Year celebration in schools or libraries, wherever I am." She then recounted a number of these celebrations that she spearheaded, from Canada to Hawaii, attracting the support of people of many different cultural backgrounds. "In Hawaii, we even had the lion dance in the public library. It was so loud!"

Flashing another smile, Amanda summed up her positive, proactive outlook by saying, "You never know until you try!"

AFTERWORD: Amanda's story illustrates the twin rewards of a playful approach when it comes to being a parent: not only are we able to engage our children more effectively in the target language through play—because play is how children are naturally wired to connect with the world—we're also able to build closer bonds with them and create warm memories that can last their whole lifetime. In fact, if we reflect on our own childhood memories of interactions with our parents, we'll likely find that many of the most glowing memories involve our parents *playing* with us in some way. Thus, playfulness not only has a very positive and productive impact on our bilingual success, those playful experiences can reverberate in our relationships with our kids and in their lives for years to come. It wouldn't surprise me at all if Amanda's children, far into the future, fondly remember that lion dance in the public library! I suppose, then, one question we might ask ourselves each busy day is this: *As I carry on with my efforts to nurture the minority language, what lasting memories would I like to create today for my kids?*

CONTACT & RESOURCES FOR AMANDA

- ✉ amanda@MissPandaChinese.com
- ⊕ MissPandaChinese.com
- ▶ youtube.com/misspandachinese
- f facebook.com/misspandachinese
- ◎ @misspandachinese
- 📖 *First Mandarin Sounds: An Awesome Chinese Word Book*
- 🔊 *Let's Learn Mandarin Chinese with Miss Panda!* (audio CD)

24

Four Children and Two Different Paths Toward Multilingual Ability

▶ Emilia is Italian and lives in Rome with her husband, Giancanio, and their four children. She is a doctor at a national health service outpatient clinic and speaks several languages besides her native Italian, including English, Spanish, and French.

▶ Giancanio works in a management role at Italy's national broadcasting company. He speaks Italian and English.

▶ Their children are Costanza, 17.1 years old; Giovanni, 15.5 years old; Bianca, 8.9 years old; and Otto, 5.9 years old.

Emilia has always had a passion for languages. Along with her native language, Italian, she has acquired good proficiency in English, Spanish, and French over the years by studying these languages and spending extended periods of time in the U.S., Spain, and France. She has also studied Portuguese and German.

"If I like something, I practice it," she said. "I read a lot, but I prefer not to read books in Italian. I choose books in foreign languages, and I keep all my favorite languages going. I'm rather methodical."

Emilia is eager to hand down her love of languages to her four children, and help nurture their multilingual ability, but she wasn't always as intentional about this aim. Referring to her two older children, she said, "I was young when they were born and I hadn't really thought about it." Even though she had gained ability in several languages, she didn't yet consider using them with her own kids. To introduce English to Costanza and Giovanni, for example, she brought them to an English school, "but the results weren't very good."

Describing the shift that took place in her thinking and her efforts, Emilia said, "The thing that put this idea in my mind was that my husband's brother lives in Madrid and his wife is Spanish. I saw his sons growing up bilingual. When they were talking to their father, they would speak Italian, and when they were talking to their mother, they would speak Spanish. So when I saw that, I said, 'I have to do it! I absolutely have to do it!'"

Along with this fresh conviction came a new realization: "Something changed in my mind and I understood that I could teach them myself. So I said, 'Let's make it like I'm a Spanish mother teaching Spanish.' I mean, not all Spanish mothers are skilled language teachers. A Spanish mother with average ability in Spanish can still teach her son the language, so why can't I do the same thing here? I have average ability. You don't need to have perfect language ability to teach it to your children."

At that point, Emilia was pregnant with her third child. "I remember trying to decide, 'Should I do this in French? Should I do it in Spanish?'" She eventually decided to use Spanish, and, with her husband behind her—but continuing to use Italian himself—she started speaking Spanish to Bianca when she was born.

Handing down her multilingual ability

Bianca's birth, then, brought the shift in attitude and action that has enabled Emilia to begin handing down her multilingual ability and passion for languages to her children—and not only the two younger children, but the two older children as well.

What Emilia discovered, as she began using Spanish with Bianca, is that Costanza and Giovanni were quickly picking up some passive ability in this language, too. When Bianca started to speak, however, she would respond to Emilia in Italian, not Spanish, because, of course, the rest of the family was communicating in Italian. It was only after they were able to place Bianca in a Spanish immersion school, at age 3, that her Spanish grew more active and became the main language for communication with Emilia.

It was around this time that the fourth child, Otto, was born. Viewing this as another opportunity to promote the multilingual life of her family, Emilia decided to introduce English into their home by speaking this language to him. "I said, 'Let's try this with English because English could be useful for the older kids in school, maybe more useful than Spanish.'"

So, for the next few years, Emilia sought to use three languages with her kids: Italian (and sometimes English) with Costanza and Giovanni, Spanish with Bianca, and English with Otto. Although she feels this period did pay off in greater passive ability in both Spanish and English for the older children, she also acknowledged that it was "messy" and hard to sustain.

Finally, when Otto was 3, and followed Bianca into the Spanish school, "English began to be left out" and her communication with him—which had been English from her and Italian from him—shifted toward using Spanish together as a shared language.

Schooling provides support for Spanish

Enrolling the two younger kids in the Spanish school, after the two older children had only been attending Italian schools, was a challenge at first, both logistically and financially. But Emilia and Giancanio persisted past the early obstacles by staying resourceful and seeking solutions. "When you're thinking about doing something, it seems so difficult," she said. "But when you actually do it, it's easier than when you were thinking about it."

And by sticking to this option for schooling, Emilia now has the support for this language that had been lacking. While she continues to speak in Spanish to Bianca and Otto, she said, "Sending them to the Spanish school has relieved me of a lot of work and a lot of worries. Before Bianca went there, I was singing, putting on CDs in Spanish, learning Spanish kids' songs. I had magazines coming, and I had a ton of books. I bought so many books! I would go to Spain once a year, at least, and buy whatever I found—books and magazines for me and for her. I would bring an empty suitcase for all that stuff!"

During these visits to Spain, Emilia would take Bianca to the playground and encourage her to listen to the other children and play with them. "I was listening myself to learn the language used for little kids, which is different from normal language. And YouTube was really useful for this, too, especially the kind of cartoons where there are children speaking."

Though Emilia is very pleased with the school, the limited class hours in Italian—just five hours a week—become a concern for many Italian families as their children get older. To gain good jobs in the future, they naturally need strong Italian. So children of Italian families often switch to Italian schools from the first year of middle school, when their children are around 11. About her own kids, she said, "We'll see, year by year."

Non-native parents improve through the process

As a non-native speaker of multiple languages that she would like to nurture in her children, Emilia encourages other non-native parents to pursue their own bilingual dream. "Many people say that they don't have a high enough level to do this. But children don't really care if you use the 's' for the third person. It's not an exam. So just do it, right or wrong, and more or less it will work."

Emilia agreed that non-native parents don't need to know everything about their target language before they embark on a bilingual journey with their kids, and in fact, this wish for perfection is unrealistic. After all, there are plenty of things—like nursery rhymes and children's songs—that even native speakers of a language aren't familiar with until they become parents. The key point is, non-native parents who pursue a bilingual aim for their children are able to become more proficient in their target language through the process itself.

"Your language ability grows if you use it," she said. "Day by day, speaking it, listening to it, reading a lot, having contact with other people, your level improves. So if you can say, 'Let's have dinner,' you say, 'Let's have dinner.' Then tomorrow you say, 'Yesterday I said only 'Let's have dinner.' So how could I say two things today?' Then the next day you say three things. I think it works like that."

Emilia admits to feeling a bit self-conscious about speaking Spanish to her children in the presence of native Spanish speakers, but doesn't let these moments of "impostor syndrome," as she called it, stop her from continuing to use this language. "In front of my family, I don't care," she said. "They think I'm crazy, anyway. So with my family, I speak it as I like. But if I speak Spanish in front of someone, I've noticed that I exaggerate my Italian accent so it's clear that I'm not trying to sound Spanish. I don't care about sounding Spanish. I just want to give the Spanish to my kids."

Two sides of the same mountain

Although Emilia and her two older children now wish they had pursued language learning with the same sort of purpose undertaken with the two younger kids, it's nevertheless true that Costanza and Giovanni have also benefited from all the exposure to Spanish and English. While their language ability is still more passive than active, with greater input and opportunity they will surely use both Spanish and English more actively in the future.

As we concluded our conversation, I told Emilia that this journey with her kids was like climbing a mountain together...except that the two older siblings and the two younger siblings are climbing up different paths, with Costanza and Giovanni on one side of the mountain and Bianca and Otto on the other side. And yet it's very possible, I said, that all four children will eventually meet at the top and attain the sort of passion and proficiency for languages that Emilia has encouraged in them over the years.

AFTERWORD: Emilia used the word "messy" to describe one stage of her bilingual journey and I was immediately reminded of a photo I once used for a blog post at Bilingual Monkeys: the image showed a small child eating a big cupcake with a messy face and a huge smile. And the caption I added beneath it read: "This cupcake might be messy, but it still tastes good." To me, that sentiment pretty much sums up the whole bilingual journey for my family and for all the families I've known because the experience inevitably feels "messy" to one degree or another. Yet even though it's "messy," it can still "taste good": it can still be successful and satisfying. You just have to keep eating! Emilia's passion for languages has powered her perseverance over the years, enabling her to continue making a range of resourceful efforts, despite missteps and setbacks, that have fueled ongoing progress for both herself and her children. What's ultimately most important for greater success, then, is the sort of genuine passion that Emilia feels because passion without know-how will still move you toward gaining the know-how you need as that passion drives you forward. But know-how without passion is like an engine without sufficient fuel and will likely lead to a lack of stamina and sustainability. The bilingual journey is a marathon, not a sprint, and deeper passion is what empowers our persistent steps through this "messy" long-term process.

25

Nurturing Good Relationships Alongside Language Ability

- ▶ Jana is originally from the Czech Republic and has lived in England for over 20 years. Bilingual in Czech and English, she works as a translator and language consultant. Her blog is called Bilingvni Vychova (bilingvni-vychova.com).

- ▶ Her husband, Steve, is British and his ability in Czech is limited. He works as an actor in casualty simulations.

- ▶ They have two children: a son, Curtis, 19 years old, and a daughter, Šárka, 16.8 years old.

- ▶ The family lives in a rural English village.

P arents with older children, like Jana, have earned a broader perspective on the bilingual journey. Looking back over the years, they can often identify some of the key principles of their quest—principles that seem to apply to so many families with a bilingual or multilingual aim.

As Jana's experience exemplifies, these include the idea that *the more that goes in, the more that eventually comes out.* In other words, the more input the child receives in the target language, from the very start, the more language he or she will be able to produce at the point when active communication begins. Moreover, that early success then creates momentum, and serves as a springboard, for continuing and expanding success.

"It's like a snowball," Jana told me in our conversation, describing how a little snowball of progress when the child is small goes on rolling and growing bigger over the years of childhood.

Proactive from the start

Jana studied English and French in the Czech Republic then came to England in 1999 to work as an au pair. After meeting Steve, the couple came to settle in a small village in southwestern England where there are no other Czechs and few people are bilingual.

While Steve has always been supportive of Jana's bilingual goal, he speaks little Czech himself. Because of this, and because the family visits the Czech Republic only once a year for a few weeks, Jana knew she would need to be very proactive to realize her aim. "I wanted my kids to be able to communicate with me in Czech," she said, "because I couldn't imagine communicating with them in English. And I wanted them to be able to communicate with my family in the Czech Republic. So my aim was communication, but I also wanted to teach them about the history and culture and literature so they not only knew the language, they knew what it meant to be Czech and they understood the Czech way of living and being, really. I guess I wanted to pass on a piece of 'Czechness' to them so they feel Czech as well as English."

When her son was born, Jana spoke to him in Czech, and only Czech. And to this day, when her children are in their late teens, she continues to speak only Czech to them; she has never used English. She told me, "Especially when you're on your own—a foreigner in a foreign country and you're the only person who speaks that language—you have to use it with them. Otherwise, they won't learn it."

Being as talkative as possible

Jana stressed the importance of being as talkative as possible, from early on, to provide young children with ample input in the minority language. "When they're really little and they can't communicate with you, you talk to yourself. I would talk to myself all the time. I would talk to myself when I was in the kitchen and Curtis was there in his baby chair. I'd be peeling potatoes and talking to him, telling him what I was doing. It might sound stupid, and it probably looks stupid, but I just somehow knew that that's what I had to do. Because if he was living in the Czech Republic, everything would be in Czech and he would be hearing it all the time, he would be immersed in it."

In this way, Jana sought to make up for that lack of immersion, to the extent she could, through her own persistent efforts to continuously "narrate" her daily experience. She explained that her parenting style would likely have been different if she had raised her children in the Czech Republic, where exposure to Czech could have come from many other sources, too. But because of her circumstances, she had to work harder to fill this dearth of general exposure to the minority language through her own actions, which began with being as talkative as possible.

"And if you're not a very talkative person," she said, "that can seem quite tough. I'm not the most talkative person in the world, either, but you just have to make yourself do it if you want your child to speak in a minority language, especially if you're the only person. If you're the only source of that language, you have to do it. You have to get used to talking out loud all the time: talk about what you're doing, what you're seeing, what you're thinking, what you're feeling. Imagine all those words that are going into their little heads. And not just the words, but the intonation and rhythm of the language. So when they're little and only a few weeks or months old, that's what's going into their heads. It's shaping their brain and it's shaping that language already."

Being talkative, she feels, was one of the main factors that fostered early success with her children, along with "lots and lots and lots" of books and reading, both fiction and nonfiction material. She noted, too, that she made a point of connecting the things they would read about with the "real world" in order to further engage them with the language and subject matter.

Creating good relationships with your kids

Jana's ability to provide her children with ample speech, since the start of her bilingual quest, has depended not only on her intentional resolve, but also on the strong relationships she has cultivated with her kids.

"You need to create a good relationship and the language will then happen through that relationship," she said. "That means spending as much time with them as you possibly can, and doing things that you both enjoy. Or doing the things that *they* enjoy because that's not necessarily going to be the same as the things that *you* enjoy."

Offering an example, Jana said that she tried getting her children to play tennis with her, which she enjoys, but it turned out that tennis didn't appeal to them. So, instead, she joined them in their own interests, going rock climbing with her son and playing football (soccer) with her daughter.

"I just love being with them, really. I never understand parents who say, when the school holidays come, 'Oh, six weeks with the kids at home! What am I going to do?' I loved it because we just enjoyed each other's company."

Jana wondered aloud why parents with a bilingual aim would send their children off to a majority language camp rather than spend time with them at home in the minority language. "You're not going to be able to pass on your language to them when you're trying to get rid of them," she said.

Maintaining communication in your language

Asked how she has been able to sustain her communication with her kids in the minority language—despite the fact that her children are clearly aware of her ability in English and don't have a natural need to use Czech with her—Jana pointed to two likely factors.

The first is connected to the close relationship that she has developed with her kids. Because of this emotional bond, which was formed in Czech, they have continued to speak Czech to her.

On top of this, she has also persisted in nurturing higher levels of Czech ability, which, as they've matured, enables them to express themselves in more sophisticated language. School, she said, can be a turning point for the use of the minority language because the majority language then grows stronger and children may no longer be able to communicate as effectively in the minority language.

"When they start school and come home with homework, I think it's important to do that homework in your minority language," she said. "But parents often find this difficult and they'll switch to the majority language, the language that the homework is written in and the kids know better because they have the vocabulary from school. In our case, though, I would always translate things into Czech. And sometimes we had to look words up in the dictionary. It's not easy, but you have to make the effort. You have to make a conscious effort to translate things into your language. Because if you start doing homework in the majority language, it can open the door for them to communicate with you in that language."

In this way, Jana not only was able to maintain Czech as their shared language, the regular efforts they made to understand the English homework *in Czech* also steadily advanced the children's ability in this language and enabled them to reach higher levels of proficiency and fluency.

Responding to kids in a fun way

While Jana has been able to sustain her children's active use of Czech, it's also true that, as they grew older, they would occasionally say something to her in English. At such moments, Jana would continue in Czech, telling them that she didn't understand English. Of course, the children knew this wasn't the case, "But I always said it in a fun way. I would never say, 'Don't speak to me in English. I don't like that.' I think you have to respond in a fun way. If you're too authoritative, they'll do it more just to annoy you. I think if you try and make it fun, they're more likely to laugh it off and do as you say and do what you want."

She continued, "I think it goes back to what we were talking about—having a good relationship with them. I think having a good relationship with your kids gives you a solid base because it just makes communication easier—as they get older, especially. When they're little, you can do pretty much what you want with them. But as they get older, especially when they start going to school and they start realizing that there's life outside the family home and they start getting other ideas and opinions, that's when having a good relationship really helps."

Snowball of success rolls onward

Despite the considerable success that Jana has achieved with her children, she admits that the original aim she held, at the very beginning, has not been fully realized. "I also wanted them to be able to read and write in Czech, correctly," she explained. "They can read. But writing is a bit more tricky. I mean, they can write in Czech, but not with perfect spelling. So we didn't quite meet that aim because, well, I'm a perfectionist and the aim was perfection! But there's still time!"

She then emphasized, though, that the idea of "perfection" can be an unrealistic goal—and a goal that can interfere with nurturing good relationships with your kids if you're pushing for "perfection" too hard. Success, she said, can still be success, even if it doesn't match all of your original objectives. At the beginning, when our children are born, we can't clearly, realistically, imagine what success will look like when they're older.

At this point, Jana feels that her bilingual journey has not only been greatly rewarding for her and for her children, it has also been a positive force in the lives of others. The extended family, on both sides, has always been very pleased that her kids are bilingual and schoolmates have viewed them in a special light because of their bilingual ability.

She even mentioned a neighbor, whose garden is adjacent to theirs, who once told her: "It's great hearing you talk in Czech with the kids. I don't have to go on holiday! I feel like I'm on holiday all the time!"

With her children now nearly young adults, the snowball of bilingual ability that has been rolling over the years, and steadily growing in size, will no doubt continue to roll onward through the rest of their lives. The idea that our kids will eventually reach the point when they take over the bilingual journey themselves, and carry on in their own way, beyond our daily involvement, is perhaps one of the final principles for all parents on this long quest.

AFTERWORD: I still vividly remember holding my daughter, our first child, in my arms on the day she was born. I know this sounds trite, but that amazing moment honestly doesn't feel very long ago...and yet she's now 17. Like Jana, I've arrived at the point where the years of diligent efforts—above all, the kind of talkative, playful spirit she stressed in her story—have paid off in strong bilingual ability that will continue to serve my kids well, long after my own daily influence has faded. It's impossible to know, of course, just how our children will make use of their language ability in the future. But chances are it will help enrich their lives in a range of meaningful ways, and benefit many others in the process, including their own kids. This is a legacy we leave behind, for our children and for the world. When our children are younger, it may be true that we're mostly focused on the present moment, and that's as it should be in order to make the most of each new day. But it's also true that those days slowly accumulate into the larger success, and the greater legacy, of this long journey. You, too, will arrive at that point much sooner than you expect. And when you do, I hope you will feel the same kind of deep satisfaction for all the rewarding distance that you and your children have traveled together.

CONTACT & RESOURCES FOR JANA

- ✉ janagarnsworthy@gmail.com
- 🌐 bilingvni-vychova.com
- f facebook.com/bilingvni.rodiny

26

Handing Down Bilingual Success, From Generation to Generation

- ▶ Delia, now in her 60s, is originally from Argentina and has lived in the U.S. for 44 years. She is fluent in Spanish and English.

- ▶ She is the mother of a bilingual daughter, Ana, now 42, and the grandmother of a bilingual granddaughter, Eva, 9.8 years old.

- ▶ Delia has worked as a medical social worker and community college administrator, and is also a writer of bilingual picture books for children and nonfiction articles (amazon.com/author/deliaberlin).

- ▶ Her parrot, Eureka, has some bilingual ability in English and Spanish, too.

We end this series of success stories with a look at Delia and her family. This time, in fact, we'll take a bird's-eye view of *generations* of a family that have roamed to various parts of the world while continuously keeping alive a through line of bilingualism in the lives of many of its members.

Delia's story reminds me of a distant past in which my own ancestors, immigrants from Europe to the U.S., led their own bilingual lives. This reality wasn't something I was clearly aware of in my youth, growing up in a monolingual family myself, but the fact remains that there has been a through line of bilingualism across generations of my own family as well. But like families everywhere, this line can become severed when the majority language dominates the daily lives of its members.

In my case, this means the bilingual ability of earlier generations was largely lost over the course of subsequent generations in the U.S., not an uncommon fate for the family tree of many American families. But now, in my own family, we have managed to pick up this thread of bilingualism again, albeit with different languages compared to the past.

Ultimately, then, sustaining or resuming the longer through line of bilingualism within a family—whatever those languages may be—depends on the actions that each family member takes during their generation's turn in the spotlight. And if bilingualism is important to a particular family member—as it clearly has been to Delia—such actions to foster bilingual ability in succeeding generations can continue to enrich the family tree with bilingualism long into the future.

From Argentina to the U.S.

While Delia is originally from Argentina, her ancestors were originally from Spain. In the 1930s, her grandparents emigrated from Spain to Argentina to seek a better life. "My grandparents were from Galicia," she said. "It's a poor, rural area in the northwest corner of Spain. In that part of Spain, people speak Gallego, a language that's closely related to Portuguese and has some influence from Castilian Spanish. My grandparents also spoke Castilian Spanish— not everyone in Galicia speaks both, but they never really valued or considered that to be bilingualism because Gallego is spoken by so few people and they were very pragmatic. They valued languages for the doors they would open."

Growing up in Argentina, Delia attended a German school, which was the product of two large waves of immigration from Germany during and after World War II. "My school was predominantly Jewish kids from families from Europe, but the kids were born in Argentina. They weren't part of an elite—most of their parents and grandparents had arrived without anything and they were small business people."

At this school, Delia learned German from first grade, English from third grade, and later in high school, French. "But academic teaching without immersion doesn't give you that much," she said.

"It gives you the basic structure of the language, but still, when I came to the U.S. in 1976, it was a steep curve for me. I was 22 and I couldn't, for example, understand or tell a joke—the nuances of languages aren't technically learned."

When Delia was 16, her family moved to Brazil for work reasons and they all acquired Portuguese. Three years later, when her father was offered a job in the U.S., her parents and three younger siblings moved to America but Delia was reluctant to join them. She had a boyfriend in Argentina, Alejandro, and wanted to remain there with him. So the two got married and Delia was able to stay. She was 19 at the time.

A few years later, however, with Argentina caught up in the turmoil of the "Dirty War," Delia and Alejandro decided to leave Argentina. "Alejandro's only brother got killed, and also several of his friends. Things were actually very terrifying in Argentina, so since my parents were living in the U.S., we left and came to Connecticut as graduate students, thinking that we would be going back when things got better in Argentina. But by the time things were better, years had passed and we had a daughter and we ended up staying."

Her daughter becomes bilingual

Delia said that, in those days, much of the information that was available about bilingualism erroneously stated that exposing a child to two languages at the same time could cause problems in language development and potentially in other areas of development as well. While she was skeptical of this warning, she moved forward with her bilingual aim for Ana by first focusing on Spanish at home and then adding English at school. "We spoke solely Spanish at home, so it was like 100% Spanish exposure for the first two years. She was extremely precocious in language so by the time she was 2 and she started at a Montessori school, she spoke more like a 4-year-old in Spanish, but she didn't speak any English. In six months, though, her English was at that level, too."

When Ana was 3, Delia's marriage to Alejandro came to an end. She then began a new relationship with an American man, David, when Ana was 4. Though David didn't speak Spanish, this significant shift in circumstances presented no real obstacles to the continuing success of Delia's bilingual journey with Ana. "By that time," Delia explained, "Ana's Spanish and English were both very well established. So if we were having a conversation with David, of course, we would speak English. But if I had to speak to Ana about anything, we would revert to Spanish whether David was there or not. He was always very understanding and supportive. He knew that it was necessary, that you really have to keep it up."

At the same time, Delia maintained a friendly relationship with Alejandro, who was living in the area, and Ana continued to spend time with him and speak Spanish when they were together. She also used Spanish with her grandparents—Delia's parents in the U.S. and Alejandro's parents in Argentina—as well as with other family members and friends there. "We would go to Argentina periodically for her to meet cousins and other children her age—to really value her skill and realize that if she didn't speak Spanish, she couldn't talk with those children."

She added, with emphasis, "I think that's really important, that the main person who has to buy into keeping the language is the child."

Difficulties along the way

While Delia was very pleased with Ana's progress in both languages, she did experience some difficulties on their bilingual journey together. She said that some people in the U.S. generalize the wide range of Spanish speakers there and this leads to stereotyping and discrimination. Sharing the impact of this negative attitude, she said, "It really worried me because I knew other children who spoke Spanish and they pretended that they didn't. It was sad that they didn't value, and didn't try to keep, a skill that could open doors for them in the future. So I wanted to pre-empt the possibility that Ana could ever feel ashamed or embarrassed of speaking Spanish by traveling and giving her opportunities to use her Spanish to help other people."

Offering an example, she said, "If I was at the grocery store with her and I noticed a Spanish-speaking family looking for a particular item, or not understanding something, instead of jumping in and helping them myself, I would encourage Ana to help them. 'Why don't you go help that lady find the raisins because she doesn't know where they are?' And so she spoke Spanish with other people in these useful ways."

At the same time that Delia sought to nurture the value and pride that Ana felt for her Spanish ability, she tried to provide similar support for other Spanish-speaking families. "The longest part of my professional career was in community college administration. I was administering a branch campus of a community college that had programs in English as a Second Language and all sorts of career programs and transfer programs—associate degrees to go on to a four-year university. And in that capacity, I was an advisor and mentor to a lot of students. Many of them were adults who were raising their own children. They were bilingual themselves, but they weren't teaching their kids Spanish because when they arrived in the U.S., they needed to learn English and without English, they couldn't survive so they didn't value their Spanish. But even when they were trying to teach their kids Spanish, the children themselves sensed that it was harder for them to succeed if they were perceived as Hispanic or Latino. So we had to counter that as much as we could."

Delia mentioned, too, that when Ana was in middle school, they encountered another kind of difficulty, one that many bilingual families experience. The Spanish classes offered at her school were far below her Spanish level, but it wasn't possible for the school to provide her with a more suitable curriculum for Spanish speakers. "Ana knew more Spanish than the teacher and she couldn't sit through classes where they were teaching the colors and the numbers," Delia said. Eventually, though, she was able to arrange with the school for Ana to work on more challenging material in the library during that time.

Delia added that Ana went on to study French in school and took part in a student exchange which enabled her to spend a summer in Wallonia, the officially French-speaking part of Belgium. And the girl she stayed with in Belgium then spent the following summer with them in the U.S. "Between the French she took in school and that experience of the student exchange, she's also pretty fluent in French."

Her granddaughter becomes bilingual

Ana, now grown, is a physician in New York City—about three hours by car from Delia—and has a daughter of her own, Eva, who is 9. Delia told me that Ana's husband, Ray, was very proactive about learning Spanish prior to Eva's arrival because the couple anticipated raising their children with a bilingual aim. So Eva's early exposure to Spanish came from both Ana and Ray, and of course, from Delia.

"When Eva was born," she explained, "I retired and I rented a small apartment very near them—around the corner—because Ana was a surgical resident at the time and her schedule was absolutely crazy. They were going to need help and they wanted me to be there as much as possible. So I would go to New York whenever she had rotations and Eva would stay with me overnight. We have very fond and funny memories of those times together. I even had a cage for Eureka there, since sometimes she made the trip with me."

In this way, Delia spent considerable time with Eva during the early years of her life. "And actually," she said, "that's when I decided to write bilingual books for children because we were constantly running out. I bought every title that was available, used up every library title that was available, and there was never enough. She loved, loved, loved to be read to."

When Eva turned 4, and started going to preschool, Delia felt that it no longer made sense to keep the apartment in New York. Since then, she has mainly spent time with Eva at her home during long weekends or school vacations. "For example, the last few years, she has gone to day camp here in Connecticut for up to two weeks at a time, and it's the same day camp that my daughter used to go to."

However, as she watched how quickly her granddaughter was growing up, Delia decided to again rent a nearby apartment in New York so she can "do more things with her one or two evenings a week or every other week."

Bilingual picture books and other writing

When I followed up on her writing, Delia told me that she has written a number of bilingual English-Spanish picture books and also contributes short stories and essays to a local publication in her area. Referring to the value of bilingual books for children, she said that such books can be useful in families where not everyone knows both languages. "For example, in Eva's case, her paternal grandparents who don't speak Spanish, or her great grandparents who didn't speak English, they could all read the same story to her. And for the child, hearing the story in both languages helps create connections between these languages from a very early age. Even for adults who are trying to learn a language, these stories can be helpful for expanding vocabulary."

While Eva enjoyed Delia's picture books when she was younger, her growing maturity and advancing reading ability have led her to appreciate her grandmother's writing for adults as well. "Many of them are kind of autobiographical," Delia said. "They talk about when I was raising Ana or when I lived in Argentina or family history."

Delia described Eva as an avid reader, in both languages, which prompted me to wonder if Delia made use of both languages, too, as a writer. "That's interesting," she said. "I can write in both languages, but it's easier for me to write in English now. If I have to compose, I'd rather compose on the keyboard in English and then translate to Spanish."

A different outcome for her siblings

I then asked about her three younger siblings in the U.S., and whether the heritage language has been handed down to their families as well. Delia shook her head and replied, "Not one of my nephews or nieces speaks Spanish. I don't fully understand what happened there. My siblings do speak Spanish, and Portuguese as well, but their spouses don't speak Spanish so maybe they found it more difficult to be the only ones speaking it."

She went on to say that her siblings have all experienced the benefits of their bilingual ability in their professional lives, and they continue to use both Spanish and Portuguese in their personal lives, too, with some family members and friends. And yet, given their circumstances, and their choices, the language of their ancestors—by way of Spain and Argentina—was not passed on to the next generation, an outcome similar to many families who have established new lives in the U.S.

A parrot with bilingual ability

An interesting sidebar to Delia's story is the fact that she has had an African Gray parrot for almost 30 years, and this parrot, named Eureka, also has a certain degree of bilingual ability in English and Spanish. Although Eureka isn't so talkative—she doesn't need to be because Delia is quite sensitive to her needs—Delia explained, "If she's fussing and I look at her like, 'What's going on?', she'll tell me, 'Wanna go see.' She wants me to take her to see something. Or she could ask for a specific food, or she might say, 'Wanna come out' or 'Want some more.' So parrots do actually have language, and I'm convinced that, in the wild, they must have different vocalizations for different things with their flock. But when they're with people, they learn to use the language that we use. She can even say our names; she can say Delia, David, and Ana."

Though Delia has only spoken English to Eureka since she was a baby—following the lead of the breeder, who was already speaking to her in English—Eureka has apparently picked up some Spanish over the years, too. "One time when a friend who I speak Spanish with came to visit, Eureka said 'Hola!' to her. She doesn't say these things very often, but she observes and remembers and can say things that are appropriate for the situation."

Whether parrots or people, language exposure is clearly the key to language acquisition and active use.

Wise advice for parents

Finally, offering some advice for parents—and grandparents—Delia made a number of important points, among them...

- "Be confident and stick to your guns. It's a good decision; no damage will come out of it."

- "Try to educate or inform the people around you, whether they are babysitters, teachers, or other relatives, to make them partners rather than adversaries in the journey."

- "Be aware of the child's attitudes toward the language and try to prevent or pre-empt any negative connotations or influence or messaging that they may be getting from any element of society. Don't let it slide—address it and explain why it's wrong to diminish the value of a language or to treat one language as less desirable than another. Any language will open doors."

She then concluded with a very wise view of the value of language ability in modern life, telling me, "And I would emphasize that with the amount of uncertainty in the world today—from economic and political reasons to climate change and the potential for displacement—you want to equip children with as many tools as you can give them for success in a variety of circumstances that you can't anticipate and languages come up very high in that."

AFTERWORD: For parents seeking to raise bilingual children, it can be difficult to see beyond the day at hand. Each day with a young child (let alone two or more kids) is so full, so busy, that it's quite understandable how a parent's perspective shrinks to a short-term view: just getting through the day, and the week, while providing ample exposure to the target language, is the most that can realistically be managed. From time to time, though, it can be very helpful, very empowering, to expand our outlook toward the months and years to come. The fact is, the efforts made today not only have a short-term impact on the child's continuing language development, they may well have a long-term impact *for decades*. And this is true not only in terms of the child's whole life ahead, as an adult, but potentially, too, when it comes to *their* children. Even further, if we look at life widely enough, we see that this influence could ripple out into the world *for generations*, far beyond our own time on this earth. In other words, there is a direct connection between today and those distant days in the future. While we may not often be mindful of this connection, especially when we're immersed in the day-to-day challenges of our lives, the profound link between the short term and long term is nevertheless true. It is *continuously* true. Delia's encouraging example can help enlarge our perspective in this way so that we're able to recall, even more keenly, how our actions in the present are not only important for the future on the near horizon, but important, too, for the farther future that we can't foresee.

CONTACT & RESOURCES FOR DELIA

- ✉ delia.berlin@gmail.com
- 🌐 amazon.com/author/deliaberlin
- 🐦 @BerlinDelia
- 📖 *Tales of Eva and Lucas – Cuentos de Eva y Lucas*
- 📖 *How to Eat a Rainbow – Cómo Comer un Arcoiris*

Final Thoughts

I began this book with a dedication to my parents. They both passed away, two months apart, in 2018.

I'll now bring the book to a close by sharing a bit more about them and the thread of bilingualism running through my own family tree, which I mentioned in the last story.

My mother and Finnish

My mother was the youngest of six children. Her parents were born in the United States, but her grandparents, on both sides, were immigrants from Finland. Her parents were bilingual in English and Finnish, while she and her siblings gained some bilingual ability to greater or lesser degrees.

Until my mother entered elementary school, her Finnish was quite active. However, after that, due to reluctance on her part to appear different from her schoolmates, as well as the fact that her parents also used English at home, her bilingual ability faded as she grew into adolescence and adulthood. By the end of her life, which she devoted to music as a church organist, pianist, and piano teacher, she could communicate very little in Finnish. However, she did have some lingering receptive skill when she heard this language.

My two siblings and I didn't receive any exposure to Finnish when we ourselves were growing up in a small city in the U.S. state of Illinois. It simply wasn't part of our lives...with the exception of a few "bad words" we pressed her to tell us.

My father and French

Meanwhile, the bilingualism on my father's side of the family had already ended in his parents' generation. My paternal grandfather was born and raised in the United States, but he apparently had difficulty communicating with his own father, who had immigrated from Romania. My grandfather spoke little Romanian, and my great-grandfather spoke little English.

As a young adult, my father, who was an artist, art professor, and musician, spent time in France as a student and a traveling folksinger. I can't really say how fluent he became in French, but he had enough confidence in his ability to attempt to speak this non-native language with his firstborn, my older brother, for the first two years of his life.

While I don't know the details of why he eventually dropped this effort, I imagine the challenges of that time, when far fewer parents were raising children in a non-native language—and no doubt there were none in our area—made this hard to sustain. In addition, my mother had little ability in French, which surely increased the level of difficulty when it came to providing language input and navigating day-to-day interactions.

The line of bilingualism

In these ways, there was both native and non-native bilingualism in my parents' lives, and there was the potential, at least, to hand down some degree of Finnish and French to me and my siblings. Yet given my family's circumstances, bilingualism simply wasn't a priority for any of us and so we grew up purely monolingual in English.

But flash forward several decades, and shift the scene from rural America to urban Japan: with my own family, bilingualism *did* become a priority. In fact, the importance of this aim was, in large part, tied right back to my parents. If I hadn't nurtured my children's English ability, my kids and their grandparents couldn't have communicated very well, and been able to create the bond that they did, while my parents were alive.

The line of bilingualism—in a brand-new form—was redrawn for my children's generation.

The spirit of success

The 26 stories in this book make it clear that success at the bilingual aim can be achieved in a world of ways. The basic challenge, for any family, involves pursuing the kinds of efforts that will be most effective, and most enjoyable, for our own particular journey. These efforts, then, will naturally vary depending on our specific circumstances and our greater goal for our children's bilingual ability. Success at language acquisition is a long continuum, from less to more language proficiency, and can include not only communicative competence but also basic literacy and even academic literacy.

Thus, every journey is inherently unique, and yet whatever our circumstances, and whatever the level of our aim, the success we seek will inevitably be linked to the same two "core conditions" of exposure and need: the child must receive ample exposure to the target language and feel a genuine need to use it actively. (Or when an organic need isn't actually present, active use of this language has been "conditioned" within the relationship.)

The line of bilingualism, that thread of language ability from one generation to the next, now continues or commences with us. It depends on our willingness to make our bilingual or multilingual aim a priority in our family's lifestyle. It depends on the actions we choose to take, day after day, to advance this aim on a gradual, ongoing basis. It depends on our patient persistence in the face of momentary setbacks or frustrations. And it depends on our enduring perseverance through the larger, long-term process of language development.

It depends, in the end, on sustaining the most mindful, proactive spirit we feel we can muster over the full length of the childhood years.

The stories in this book, as well as the millions of other stories now being lived by the world's bilingual and multilingual families, show that success can be realized by all who truly seek it.

May your story be a success story, too.

Quick Finder

STORY	AGE OF CHILDREN	CURRENT LOCATION	PARENTS ORIGINALLY FROM	LANGUAGES	OTHER	CONTACT
1 (p. 13)	3.2	U.S.	Spain	English, Spanish, German, French	Single parent	p. 19
2 (p. 21)	3	China	China The Czech Republic	Mandarin, Chinese dialect, Czech, English		p. 27
3 (p. 29)	3.5 10 months	U.S.	Brazil Ukraine	English, Portuguese, Russian		p. 37
4 (p. 39)	4.9 3.1	Poland	Poland	Polish, English	Non-native speaker	p. 46
5 (p. 47)	5.2	U.S.	U.S. Pakistan	English, Arabic, Urdu		p. 54
6 (p. 55)	5.4 3.3	UK	UK Italy	English, Italian, Spanish		p. 60
7 (p. 61)	6.3 3.3	Spain	Spain	Spanish, English	Non-native speaker	
8 (p. 71)	6 3.5	Denmark	Denmark Mongolia	Danish, Mongolian, English		
9 (p. 83)	7.2 3.6	France	France Spain	French, Spanish, English		p. 89
10 (p. 91)	7.2 4.5	U.S.	U.S. Brazil	English, Portuguese	Homeschooling	p. 99
11 (p. 101)	7.4	U.S.	U.S. India	English, Hindi, Spanish		p. 108
12 (p. 109)	8.8 5.8	U.S.	U.S. Colombia	English, Spanish		p. 116
13 (p. 117)	9.2	France	France Germany	French, German, English		p. 124
14 (p. 125)	10.6 4.6	UK	Poland	English, Polish		p. 130

STORY	AGE OF CHILDREN	CURRENT LOCATION	PARENTS ORIGINALLY FROM	LANGUAGES	OTHER	CONTACT
15 (p. 131)	10.6 7.3	U.S.	U.S. Russia	English, Russian, Spanish		
16 (p. 139)	10.9 7.11 4.11 1.9	U.S.	U.S. Thailand	English, French, Lao	Non-native speaker	p. 146
17 (p. 147)	10.11 7.5 4.6	Germany	Germany Spain	German, Spanish, English		p. 155
18 (p. 157)	11.1 8.3	U.S.	U.S. Hungary	English, Hungarian	Homeschooling	p. 164
19 (p. 165)	11 9.4	U.S.	U.S. Brazil	English, Portuguese		p. 173
20 (p. 175)	12.5 10.6	Japan	Japan UK	Japanese, English	Special needs	p. 182
21 (p. 185)	13.9 11.6	France	France U.S.	French, English		p. 192
22 (p. 193)	16.8 13.3 (twins)	The Netherlands	Italy Switzerland	Dutch, German, English, Swiss German, Italian, French, Spanish		p. 199
23 (p. 201)	16.1 14.3	U.S.	U.S. Taiwan	English, Mandarin		p. 206
24 (p. 207)	17.1 15.5 8.9 5.9	Italy	Italy	Italian, Spanish, English	Non-native speaker	
25 (p. 213)	19 16.8	UK	UK The Czech Republic	English, Czech		p. 219
26 (p. 221)	9.8 (grandchild)	U.S.	Argentina (grandparent)	English, Spanish	Grandparent & grandchild	p. 229

Acknowledgments

Fittingly, a book which shares stories from around the world was realized only through the contributions of so many people worldwide.

First and foremost, I want to offer my immense thanks, once more, to all the parents who kindly agreed to speak with me at length about your bilingual or multilingual lives as a family. I'm very grateful for your participation, whether or not your story appears in this book, and not only for sharing your experiences with me so candidly but also for providing such helpful feedback on the completed manuscript. While I won't attempt to list every individual name, please know that my appreciation is indeed heartfelt for each one of you.

I'd also like to spotlight the generous support of all those who were donors at my Patreon page. You helped make my marvelous trip to Europe possible in the fall of 2019. Among these supporters were Josh Selig, MeiHui Wu, Deborah Terhune, Mari Jose Serrano, Angela Jane Hundley, Undraa Enkhjin, Sarah Bizaj, Lyn Tobari, Vaishali Prazmari, and Małgorzata Wiśniewska. Many thanks to all of you, and to all the rest of my kind supporters at Patreon.

Thank you, as well, to Justine Montaray for transcribing the many interviews that I recorded. Your hard work enabled me to focus on writing the book with full transcripts in hand. When it was finally ready to go into production, Mario Marić lent his designer's eye to make the book look beautiful. And Donnie Obina, the world's finest illustrator of bearded dragons, contributed his creative skill for the cover image.

I'm also grateful for the enriching camaraderie of the many parents I've interacted with over the years, online and off, and my colleagues in this field, whose work has continuously helped make my own work stronger. Let me mention my appreciation, in particular, for the long-running support of Annick De Houwer, who wrote the lovely foreword for this book, and François Grosjean.

To all those who offered words of encouragement over the several years it took to produce this book, thank you. Every message I received through my blog, forum, email, or social media was truly appreciated.

And finally, my lasting gratitude to my wife and my kids, who have been the basis for my own family's bilingual journey and the foundation for all my efforts to support other families with a bilingual or multilingual dream.

About the Author

A dam Beck is the author of the popular books *Maximize Your Child's Bilingual Ability* and *Bilingual Success Stories Around the World*, both praised worldwide by parents and leaders in the field of child bilingualism for their practical and empowering approach to the bilingual aim. He is also the author of the playful "picture book for adults" titled *I WANT TO BE BILINGUAL!* (illustrated by Pavel Goldaev), which emphasizes the most important information parents need for realizing joyful success on a bilingual journey.

In addition, he created *28 Bilingual English-Spanish Fairy Tales & Fables*, a language learning resource containing short, simple texts on dual-facing English and Spanish pages. This engaging book, with online audio, is useful for any learner of Spanish or English, from kids to adults.

Adam is the founder of the influential blog Bilingual Monkeys and the lively forum The Bilingual Zoo. Along with his books and his online writing, he provides empowering support to bilingual and multilingual families through personal coaching, online and off, and through speaking appearances at conferences and workshops worldwide. He is on the consultation team at the Harmonious Bilingualism Network (HaBilNet), led by Annick De Houwer.

An educator for over 30 years, Adam has worked with hundreds of bilingual and multilingual children as a classroom teacher and private tutor. Originally from the United States, he has lived in Hiroshima, Japan since 1996 and is raising two trilingual children in Japanese, English, and Spanish. He attended college in New York, graduate school in San Francisco, and was a Peace Corps Volunteer in the Czech Republic, where he taught English at the University of West Bohemia in the city of Plzeň.

Adam also has a background in theater arts and worked for many years in children's theater as a director and playwright. He is the author of the award-winning humorous novel for children and adults titled *How I Lost My Ear* (illustrated by Simon Farrow), which critics have called "an extraordinary imaginative achievement" and compared to "the best of Roald Dahl."

Postscript

If you found value in this book, perhaps others would, too. Please kindly share your impressions with others, online and off.

- Share the book with your local community.

- Share the book on social media.

- Share the book on blogs, forums, and Facebook groups.

- Share the book in online reviews at Amazon and Goodreads.

- Share the book by gifting it to other parents and to your local library.

Your support would be truly appreciated. And if I can be helpful to this in some way—by joining you for an interview, offering images, providing a copy of the book for a giveaway, etc.—don't hesitate to reach out to me.

adam@bilingualmonkeys.com

Thank you so much!

Made in the USA
Las Vegas, NV
22 September 2023

77912011R00148